TACO
NIGHT

KATE McMILLAN

PHOTOGRAPHS BY ERIN KUNKEL

weldon**owen**

CONTENTS

TACOS FOR DINNER

If you want a foolproof way to please friends and family, let them know that it's taco night! Everyone loves to load up their favorite wraps with hearty fillings, flavorful toppings, zesty sauces, and more. The create-your-own nature of tacos makes them an easy and satisfying dinnertime solution.

In these pages, you'll find dozens of recipes for homemade tacos. Many of the dishes come together quickly on a stovetop, and others feature protein and vegetables cooked on the grill. While some recipes require minimal prep work—little more than seasoning a can of beans and chopping a few vegetables—others have the taco purist in mind: homemade corn tortillas, house-pickled chiles, and restaurant-quality seasoned meats.

Tacos appeal to all ages and offer an easy way to accommodate both dietary needs and personal preferences at the table. For example, gluten-free eaters can use lettuce cups or pure corn tortillas as their preferred wrap. Vegetarians will like the chapter dedicated to vegetable- and bean-based creations. There are also plenty of fresh new recipes for anyone who enjoys meat, poultry, and fish, as well as a chapter devoted to easy sides and salads to round out any meal.

Tacos are also a great choice for entertaining. In the warm-weather months, load up the grill with your favorite ingredients for fillings—anything from hunks of meat or poultry to a whole fish—and offer a selection of vegetables and soft tortillas. Set up a taco bar with an array of diverse toppings, sauces, and sides so that everyone can customize their own tacos. Salsas and toppings can be made ahead of time and refrigerated, and many of the other key ingredients are probably already in your refrigerator or pantry. Tacos are also an excellent way to use a wide array of leftovers. Leftover cooked meat or chicken from one night's dinner can be shredded or cubed and used as a quick filling the next night. Add a pot of rice or a few shaved raw vegetables to make it a meal.

The next time you reach for a take-out menu on a busy weeknight, or scramble for a dinner party idea, look to this inspiring cookbook for recipes that everyone will enjoy.

ANATOMY OF A TACO

Well-seasoned fillings, warm tortillas, fresh toppings, and spicy sauces—these are the ingredients that make up a perfect taco. Each element offers a multitude of possibilities, so you can customize your meal as you like. A taco can be as simple as a warmed corn tortilla wrapped around spiced black beans with a spoonful of purchased salsa, or as special as a homemade corn tortilla stuffed with grilled marinated pork and diced fresh pineapple. Here are a few tips to get you started.

THE FILLING

The most important part of a taco is the filling and should be the first thing to consider. It will help determine both the type of wrap and toppings. Proteins, such as meat, chicken, fish, beans, and tofu are all great options, but vegetables, eggs, and cheese are also satisfying and delicious. Because the filling is the highlight of the taco, the choice of seasoning is important.

THE WRAP

Whether a soft corn or flour tortilla, a crispy shell, or even a lettuce cup, the wrap should complement the filling. Grilled meats such as steak, chicken, or marinated pork are ideal wrapped in soft tortillas. Softer fillings, such as chorizo and grilled fish, work well tucked in a crispy taco shell or a crisp lettuce cup. When serving tacos in soft tortillas, whether corn or flour, be sure to warm them before serving.

THE TOPPINGS

Crunchy shredded lettuce or cabbage, pickled vegetables, fresh herbs, fiery jalapeño slices, and shredded cheese in any combination enhance tacos. These items boost flavor and add both nutrition and color.

THE SAUCES

From fresh salsas to creamy guacamole, hot chile sauces to cooling crema, there are lots of taco sauces to choose from. Set out bowls of different sauces so diners can personalize the flavors in their taco. Spice lovers can amp up the heat with chile-based salsas, while those who prefer a mellower meal might add crema or guacamole.

TACO PRIMER

There are almost no hard-and-fast rules when it comes to making tacos. You can prepare everything from scratch, swap in purchased items, or employ a combination of homemade and store-bought elements. Here are some guidelines to help you create perfect tacos, every time.

MARINATE FOR FLAVOR Marinating meats, poultry, fish, tofu, or vegetables adds bold flavor and, in some cases, has a tenderizing effect.

SELECT THE BEST Whether you're shopping for fresh ingredients or selecting premade items like jarred salsa and packaged tortillas, choose the best quality possible to ensure tasty results. Fresh herbs, ripe seasonal vegetables, quality cheeses, pastured meats and poultry, and wild fish from a sustainable source are all good options.

PREP YOUR INGREDIENTS To put dinner together quickly, have all your ingredients and tools laid out before firing up the grill or turning on the stove. Many salsas and sauces can be made ahead, saving you time when it comes to getting dinner on the table. Then chop your ingredients, grate your cheese, and get cooking.

WARM THE TORTILLAS Tortillas taste best when warmed. If grilling the taco filling, place the tortillas directly on the grate and warm them for about 2 minutes on each side. If cooking indoors, heat tortillas in a dry skillet over medium heat for about 2 minutes on each side, or wrap in aluminum foil and heat in a warm oven for 5–10 minutes. After heating tortillas, wrap them in a clean kitchen towel to keep them warm until ready to use.

BE BOLD Don't hold back on bold flavors. Customize the spiciness of tacos by adding more or less chiles or hot spices. Draw on ingredients and seasonings like fresh cilantro, lime juice, salt, and pepper to enhance the flavor; if the filling is mild, try a pepper-spiked cheese, fiery salsa, and chopped herbs or raw chiles.

MAKE THEM YOUR OWN Tacos are easy to customize, which makes them a great option for picky eaters and for big gatherings. Set out each of the taco components separately and let diners assemble their own.

TOOLS FOR SUCCESS

These basic tools will help you create foolproof taco dinners.

GRILLING TONGS & SPATULA A long-handled, heatproof set of tongs and a spatula will make easy work of flipping and transferring food when grilling.

DEEP-FRYING THERMOMETER Whether frying tortillas for crisp taco shells or cooking battered fish fillets, a deep-frying thermometer will ensure consistent results.

FOOD PROCESSOR A food processor is ideal for blending quick marinades, salsas, cremas, and more. Shredding and slicing blades come in handy for prepping large amounts of cheese and vegetables. Some processors come with different blades or they can be purchased with the model.

TORTILLA PRESS If you enjoy the flavor and texture of homemade tortillas, a tortilla press comes in handy. A rolling pin also does the trick.

BRINGING IT ALL TOGETHER

Having the taco ingredients prepped in advance helps the process go smoothly and efficiently. Measure out ingredients ahead of time before preparing fillings and sauces. When ready to assemble the tacos, have the tortillas warmed and the sauces and toppings ready to go.

TACO TIMELINE

1 DAY BEFORE Make the salsa or sauce.

A FEW HOURS OR THE NIGHT BEFORE Marinate any ingredients if called for in the recipe.

30 MINUTES BEFORE If necessary, fire up the grill or preheat the oven (to warm the tortillas). Prep your toppings: shred the cheese, chop fresh herbs and vegetables, and quarter limes.

15 MINUTES BEFORE Warm the tortillas and/or beans and start grilling or sautéing fillings.

5 MINUTES BEFORE Lay out all the taco elements for assembly.

TACO TIME! Let diners make their own tacos and enjoy!

MAKE IT A MEAL

Tacos can easily be bulked up to provide a hearty and well-rounded meal.

MAKE A TACO SALAD To transform a taco into a salad, add a handful or two of your favorite chopped lettuces or greens to an individual plate. Chop the filling and toppings of your taco together (omit the tortilla), then layer it on top of the greens. Use the salsa as a dressing or make a simple vinaigrette from olive oil and lime juice. Add crumbled tortilla chips for crunch.

ADD RICE & BEANS This classic side dish duo can be served alongside any kind of taco to add more volume to the meal. Make them yourself or purchase them at a local taqueria.

PUT AN EGG ON IT A fried egg is a delicious and protein-rich addition to any vegetarian taco.

GRILLED VEGETABLES If you are grilling your filling, throw on some extra vegetables, such as corn, zucchini, onions, or whatever is in season and serve as an additional topping.

SHORTCUTS FOR A BUSY DAY

Look for these good-quality premade taco elements to help get dinner on the table quickly and easily during the week.

SALSAS Purchase jarred salsas and hot sauces for easy assembly. For the closest to homemade, look for fresh salsa at upscale markets or pick up the house sauce from your favorite local Mexican restaurant.

CHEESE & TOPPINGS Save time and labor by using a food processor to shred cheese and lettuce, cabbage, or other vegetables the night before your meal and store in zippered plastic bags in the refrigerator.

TORTILLAS Ask your local taqueria if they sell homemade tortillas or prepared masa dough that you can press and cook at home.

SIDES & SALADS Purchase premade side dishes or salads from your local market or deli. A bowl of fresh greens, like arugula or baby kale, tossed with orange segments and drizzled with olive oil and vinegar makes a simple side salad.

WEEKEND TACO PARTY

The weekend is the perfect time to invite a few friends over for a taco fiesta. Keep it fun and casual with a taco bar that invites guests to get creative with their choices.

MAKE 1–3 SAUCES IN ADVANCE Pico de Gallo (page 20) and Fire-Roasted Tomato Salsa (page 22) are classic crowd-pleasers and can easily be made ahead. Prepare fruit and avocado-based sauces just before guests arrive.

SET OUT A VARIETY OF ITEMS A selection of fillings—meat, poultry, fish, or beans—plus fresh vegetables, salsas, a pot of Mexican rice, and plenty of limes, cilantro, and pickled red onions guarantee countless options for taco creations.

SET UP A BUFFET Start with plates and utensils, then leave space for warm tortillas (set these out at the last minute). Arrange taco components in the order that guests will add them to their tacos. First, set out the main fillings and include a variety of vegetarian and non-vegetarian options. Then offer different fresh toppings, followed by a selection of crumbled or shredded cheeses. Finally, set out the salsas or sauces and guacamole at the end of the buffet.

POTLUCK PARTY Ask guests to bring their favorite side dish, salsa, or tortilla chips.

PARTY DRINKS Make a large batch of agua frescas or pitchers of limeade. Chill Mexican-style beer in a galvanized tub of ice. Set out a bottle of white tequila and lime wedges for guests to create cocktails.

ESSENTIALS

3 ripe avocados, halved and pitted

3 tablespoons chopped fresh cilantro

Juice of 1 lime

1 or 2 dashes of hot sauce, such as Tabasco (optional)

Kosher salt and freshly ground pepper

TAQUERIA GUACAMOLE

Scoop the flesh from the avocados into a bowl. Using a potato masher or a large fork, smash the avocados until mostly smooth. Stir in the cilantro, lime juice, and hot sauce, if using. Season with salt and pepper and serve right away. To store, cover the bowl tightly with plastic wrap so that the plastic is touching the guacamole and refrigerate for up to 1 day.

MAKES ABOUT 2 CUPS (16 OZ/500 G)

VARIATIONS

CHUNKY GUACAMOLE Pit, peel, and cut 3 avocados into ½-inch (12-mm) cubes and place in a bowl. Add 2 ripe plum (Roma) tomatoes, cut into small dice; 3 tablespoons finely chopped red onion; ¼ cup (⅓ oz/10 g) chopped fresh cilantro; the juice of 1 lime; and 1 small jalapeño chile, seeded and minced. Gently toss. Season with salt and pepper.

AVOCADO CREMA Scoop the flesh from 1 avocado, halved and pitted, into a small bowl and mash with a large fork until creamy and smooth. Stir in ¼ cup (2 oz/60 g) Mexican crema or sour cream and 1 tablespoon fresh lime juice. Season with salt and serve right away.

AVOCADO LOVE

Avocados have been hailed as Mexico's gift to the world. They're delicious mashed into creamy guacamole or cubed and scattered over tacos and nachos. Plus, avocados are chock-full of good-for-you fats. When selecting an avocado, carefully pop off the button-like brown piece on the stem end. The color underneath should be green, revealing that the avocado is or will soon be ripe.

3 large, ripe tomatoes (about 1 lb/500 g), finely chopped and seeded

½ white onion, finely chopped

¼ cup (⅓ oz/10 g) loosely packed fresh cilantro leaves, chopped

1 jalapeño chile, seeded and minced

2 cloves garlic, minced

Juice of 1 lime

Kosher salt and freshly ground pepper

PICO DE GALLO

GOES WITH EVERYTHING

>>>>>>>>>>>

This classic fresh salsa adds kick to any Latin dish. Use it as a topping for tacos, a dip for tortilla chips, or as an extra layer of flavor atop beans or rice. Choose tomatoes at the peak of their season and give the salsa time to stand (up to 24 hours) to develop more flavor.

In a nonreactive bowl, stir together the tomatoes, onion, cilantro, jalapeño, garlic, and lime juice. Season with salt and pepper. Let the salsa stand at room temperature for at least 15 minutes, stirring once or twice. Serve right away or store in an airtight container in the refrigerator for up to 5 days.

MAKES ABOUT 2½ CUPS (15 OZ/470 G)

1 lb (500 g) ripe plum (Roma) tomatoes

1 jalapeño chile

3 cloves garlic, unpeeled

½ white onion, quartered

2 teaspoons olive oil

⅓ cup (½ oz/15 g) loosely packed fresh cilantro leaves, chopped

1 teaspoon red wine vinegar

Kosher salt

FIRE-ROASTED TOMATO SALSA

SMOKY & FLAVORFUL

A quick turn under the broiler gives vegetables a deep smoky flavor that adds to the intensity of this salsa. Turn this into grilled salsa by placing the vegetables over direct heat on a grill. During the winter months, substitute 1 can (14½ oz/455 g) of fire-roasted tomatoes for the fresh tomatoes.

Preheat the broiler. Line a baking sheet with aluminum foil.

Cut the tomatoes in half lengthwise and arrange on the prepared pan, cut side down. Place the jalapeño, garlic, and onion on the pan so everything is in a single, uncrowded layer. Drizzle with the olive oil. Slip under the broiler about 6 inches (15 cm) from the heat source and broil, turning the vegetables once and rotating the pan as needed, until the vegetables are charred all over, about 5 minutes per side. Remove from the oven and let cool.

When cool enough to handle, seed the jalapeño and peel the garlic. Combine the tomatoes, jalapeño, garlic, onion, and cilantro in a blender or food processor. Process until well combined and there are no large chunks left, but the salsa still has plenty of texture. Add the vinegar and pulse to combine. Season with salt. Serve right away or store in an airtight container in the refrigerator for up to 1 week.

MAKES ABOUT 1¾ CUPS (10½ OZ/330 G)

1 lb (500 g) freshly prepared masa or
1¾ cups (9 oz/280 g) masa harina

1 teaspoon sea salt

1 cup (8 fl oz/250 ml) plus 2 tablespoons
warm water, as needed

CORN TORTILLAS

If using fresh masa, put the masa in a bowl and knead with the salt, adding a little warm water, if needed, to soften it. If using masa harina, put it in a bowl, add the warm water, and mix with your hands. Allow the dough to rest for 5 minutes, then add the salt and knead for 1 minute. Shape the dough into golf ball–sized balls, then cover with a damp kitchen towel. Using a tortilla press or a rolling pin, flatten the dough into thin disks.

Heat a cast-iron frying pan or a large griddle over medium heat. One at a time, carefully slide the tortillas into the hot pan. Cook, turning once, until freckled, about 30 seconds per side. Transfer to a plate and cover with a kitchen towel to keep warm.

MAKES ABOUT TEN 5-INCH (13-CM) TORTILLAS

VARIATION

CRISPY TACO SHELLS Pour ½ cup (4 fl oz/125 ml) canola oil into a small frying pan and heat to 365°F (185°C) on a deep-frying or candy thermometer. (If you don't have a thermometer, your best test is to dip the edge of a tortilla into the oil; it should sizzle immediately and vigorously.)

Using tongs, carefully add the tortillas, 1 at a time, to the pan and cook for 15 seconds per side. Using tongs, fold over one half of the tortilla and hold it so only the bottom half is in the oil for 30 seconds. Repeat on the other side to form a shell. Carefully transfer the shell to a plate lined with paper towels to drain. Sprinkle with salt and serve.

FLATTEN 'EM OUT

Tortilla is Spanish for "little cake" and they are a staple of the Mexican diet, eaten at virtually every meal. While it is easiest to make a corn tortilla using a tortilla press, you can also use a rolling pin or flatten small balls of dough between two plates. Flattening the tortillas is a great way to get the kids involved in the kitchen. Store homemade corn tortillas wrapped in a clean kitchen towel for up to 1 day, then wrap in plastic and refrigerate for up to 4 days longer.

2 tablespoons olive oil

Zest and juice of 1 lime

1 teaspoon honey

1 clove garlic, minced

1 small jalapeño chile, seeded and minced

Kosher salt and freshly ground pepper

1 cup (3 oz/90 g) shredded green cabbage

1 cup (3 oz/90 g) shredded red cabbage

1 large carrot, shredded (about ¾ cup/ 4 oz/125 g)

TANGY COLESLAW

CRUNCHY VEGGIE TOPPING

→→→→→→→→→→

Here's a great way to get vegetables into your kid's tacos! Whether you like your coleslaw tangy or creamy, it adds an irresistible crunch to a taco. Because cabbage is so dense, it can be dressed well ahead of time and still hold its crunch. You can also try other vegetables in a coleslaw such as shredded brussels sprouts, kale, or broccoli.

In a large bowl, stir together the olive oil, lime zest and juice, honey, garlic, and jalapeño. Season well with salt and pepper.

Stir in the cabbages and carrot and toss until well coated with the dressing. Let the slaw stand at room temperature for about 10 minutes, stir again, and serve right away.

MAKES ABOUT 2½ CUPS (10 OZ/315 G)

VARIATION

CREAMY CILANTRO SLAW In a large bowl, stir together 3 tablespoons mayonnaise, 1 teaspoon distilled white vinegar, the garlic, and the jalapeño and season with salt and pepper. Add the cabbages, carrot, and ½ cup (¾ oz/20 g) loosely packed fresh chopped cilantro. Gently toss and serve right away.

WHAT YOU NEED

1 lb (500 g) tomatillos, papery husks removed

1 serrano chile

3 cloves garlic, unpeeled

½ white onion, finely chopped

½ cup (¾ oz/20 g) loosely packed fresh cilantro leaves

Kosher salt

SALSA VERDE

Preheat the broiler. Line a baking sheet with aluminum foil.

Rinse the tomatillos under warm water to dissolve the sticky coating on the skins. Pat dry, cut in half lengthwise, and arrange on the prepared pan, cut side down. Place the serrano and garlic on the pan so everything is in a single, uncrowded layer. Slip under the broiler about 6 inches (15 cm) from the heat source and broil, turning everything once and rotating the pan as needed, until the vegetables are charred all over, 4 or 5 minutes per side. Remove from the oven and let cool.

When cool enough to handle, remove the stem from the chile and peel the garlic. Combine the tomatillos, serrano, garlic, onion, cilantro, and ½ teaspoon salt in a blender or food processor and process to a coarse purée. Taste and adjust the seasoning and serve right away or store in an airtight container in the refrigerator for up to 1 week.

MAKES ABOUT 2½ CUPS (15 OZ/470 G)

TOMATILLO PRIMER

This green salsa gets its color form the tomatillos and its spicy flair from the serrano chile. When choosing tomatillos, pick ones that have a fresh-looking paper husk for the best flavor. If the husk looks dried and wrinkled, the tomatillos are probably not fresh. Tomatillos are at their peak in late summer. Store them in paper husks until ready to use.

½ pineapple, peeled, cored, and diced (about 2½ cups/15 oz/470 g)

1 cup (5 oz/155 g) peeled and diced jicama

½ cup (¾ oz/20 g) loosely packed fresh cilantro leaves, chopped

⅓ cup (1¾ oz/50 g) finely chopped red onion

1 small jalapeño chile, seeded and minced

2 tablespoons olive oil

1 tablespoon fresh lime juice

Kosher salt and freshly ground pepper

PINEAPPLE-JICAMA SALSA

In a nonreactive bowl, gently toss together the pineapple, jicama, cilantro, onion, jalapeño, olive oil, and lime juice. Season with salt and pepper. Let the salsa stand at room temperature for about 15 minutes, stirring once or twice. Serve right away or store in an airtight container in the refrigerator for up to 1 day.

MAKES ABOUT 3½ CUPS (21 OZ/655 G)

VARIATION

WATERMELON-JALAPEÑO SALSA In a nonreactive bowl, gently toss together 2½ cups (15 oz/470 g) small cubes seedless watermelon, the cilantro, onion, jalapeño, olive oil, and the zest and juice of 1 lime. Season with salt and pepper and serve right away.

PUT SOME FRUIT ON IT

Fruit salsas add a wonderful sweet, cooling component to spicy tacos, as well as a healthy dose of color and vitamins. Peaches, nectarines, mangoes, or watermelon can replace the pineapple. Because of their high liquid content, these salsas don't last long. For the freshest taste and appearance, aim to make the salsa no more than 1 hour before serving.

1½ cups (12 fl oz/375 ml) distilled white vinegar

¼ cup (2 oz/60 g) sugar

½ teaspoon kosher salt

1 bay leaf

5 peppercorns

3 jalapeño chiles, cut into ⅛-inch (3-mm) slices

1 large carrot, peeled and cut on the diagonal into ¼-inch (6-mm) slices (about 1 cup/ 4 oz/125 g)

½ red onion, sliced

PICKLED JALAPEÑOS & CARROTS

A POP OF HEAT

>>>>>>>>>

Also called escabeche, this dish is served as a condiment at many Mexican meals. Set it out with your tacos and let guests add as they please. The best part about this incredibly flavorful recipe is that the pickles only get better with time, so make this well in advance. Keep in mind that the jalapeños only mellow slightly in the liquid.

Combine the vinegar, sugar, salt, bay leaf, and peppercorns in a heavy-bottomed saucepan over medium heat and cook, stirring once or twice, until the sugar and salt dissolve, about 2 minutes.

Add the jalapeños, carrot, and onion and reduce the heat to low. Cook, stirring occasionally, until the vegetables are soft, about 1½ hours. Using a slotted spoon, transfer the pickles to a serving bowl and let cool. Serve right away or store in an airtight container in the refrigerator, with enough pickling liquid to cover, for up to 2 weeks.

MAKES ABOUT 3 CUPS (18 OZ/560 G)

VARIATION

PICKLED RED ONIONS In a nonreactive bowl, whisk together 6 tablespoons (3 fl oz/ 90 ml) rice wine vinegar, 1 tablespoon sugar, and 1½ teaspoons kosher salt until the sugar and salt dissolve. Add 1 large red onion, quartered and thinly sliced lengthwise, and toss to coat. Let stand at room temperature, stirring occasionally, for about 30 minutes. Use right away or store in an airtight container in the refrigerator for up to 2 weeks.

TACOS

meat • seafood • vegetarian

WHAT YOU NEED

3 cups (24 fl oz/750 ml) low-sodium beef broth, plus more as needed

4 dried ancho chiles

2 tablespoons olive oil

5 lb (2.5 kg) bone-in beef short ribs

Kosher salt and freshly ground pepper

1 yellow onion, finely chopped

4 cloves garlic, minced

1 cup (8 fl oz/250 ml) dry red wine

16–20 flour or corn tortillas, warmed

Pickled Red Onions (page 30), for serving

1 cup (8 oz/250 g) Mexican crema, sour cream, or crème fraîche

Fresh cilantro leaves for serving

ANCHO SHORT RIB TACOS WITH PICKLED RED ONIONS

Preheat the oven to 350°F (180°C). In a saucepan over high heat, bring the broth to a boil, then remove from the heat and add the chiles. Set aside to steep.

Warm the olive oil in a heavy-bottomed, ovenproof pot over medium-high heat. Season the short ribs all over with salt and pepper. Working in batches, add the ribs to the pot and sear until browned on all sides, about 4 minutes per side. Transfer to a plate and set aside. Add the onion to the pot and cook, stirring often, until golden, about 4 minutes. Add the garlic, season with salt and pepper, and cook just until the garlic is soft, about 1 minute. Add the broth, chiles, and wine, stirring to scrape up any browned bits on the bottom of the pot. Nestle the ribs in the liquid, cover the pot, and transfer to the oven. Bake until the meat falls off the bones, 2½–3 hours. Check the pot every 45 minutes or so to make sure there is enough liquid, adding more broth as needed; it should reach about three-fourths of the way up the sides of the ribs.

Using tongs, transfer the ribs and the chiles to a plate to cool. Set the pot with the cooking liquid aside to cool. When cool enough to handle, using your hands or 2 forks, shred the meat and set aside. Discard the bones. Using a large spoon, skim the fat off the top of the cooled liquid in the pot. Transfer the contents of the pot and 1 of the chiles to a blender and process to a smooth purée. Return the puréed sauce to the pot and bring to a boil over high heat. Cook until the sauce reduces by half, about 5 minutes. Add the shredded meat and cook just until warmed through, about 4 minutes.

To assemble, fill the tortillas with the meat and top with some drained pickled onions, a dollop of crema, and some cilantro. Serve right away.

SERVES 6–8

WORTH THE WAIT

It takes a long time in the oven to cook, but the rich flavors of fork-tender ribs combined with cooling Mexican crema and tart, crunchy pickled red onions make for a sensational taco. The ancho short ribs are so mouthwatering tender, you'll want to make a double batch and freeze half for a later use. Extra meat is delicious tucked into quesadillas, topped on nachos, or as the meat layer in a Mexican-inspired eggs Benedict.

3 cloves garlic, minced

1 jalapeño chile, seeded and minced

½ cup (¾ oz/20 g) loosely packed fresh cilantro leaves, chopped

Juice of 2 limes

Juice of 1 orange

5 tablespoons (3 fl oz/80 ml) olive oil

2 tablespoons distilled white vinegar

Kosher salt and freshly ground pepper

2 lb (1 kg) flank steak

2 large yellow onions, thinly sliced

10–12 corn or flour tortillas, warmed

Pico de Gallo (page 20)

CARNE ASADA WITH CARAMELIZED ONIONS

SEARED & CARAMELIZED

>>>>>>>>>

Here, beefy flank steak is imbued with a sweet and spicy citrus marinade before being seared on the grill. The citrus in the marinade helps the steak caramelize on the grill, producing a sweet flavor that complements the caramelized onions. Serve these tacos with a green salad, such as Butter Lettuce, Papaya & Avocado Salad (page 112).

In a bowl, whisk together the garlic, jalapeño, cilantro, lime juice, orange juice, 3 tablespoons of the olive oil, the vinegar, and 1 teaspoon salt. Place the flank steak in a large zippered plastic bag and pour in the marinade. Let marinate in the refrigerator, turning the bag once or twice, for at least 2 hours and up to 8 hours.

To make the caramelized onions, warm the remaining 2 tablespoons olive oil in a frying pan over high heat. Add the onions and sauté until translucent, about 5 minutes. Reduce the heat to medium-low and season well with salt and pepper. Cook slowly, stirring occasionally, until the onions turn a very deep brown, 35–45 minutes. Set aside and cover to keep warm.

Meanwhile, build a medium-hot fire in a charcoal grill or preheat a gas grill to medium-high.

Coat the grill grate lightly with cooking spray. Remove the steak from the marinade and let stand at room temperature for 15 minutes. (Discard the marinade.) Arrange the steak on the grate directly over the heat and grill, turning once, until nicely grill-marked and cooked to the desired doneness, about 5 minutes per side for medium-rare. Transfer the steak to a cutting board, cover loosely with aluminum foil, and let rest for about 10 minutes. Carve the steak across the grain on the diagonal into ¼-inch (6-mm) slices.

To assemble, fill the tortillas with the steak and top with the caramelized onions. Serve right away, passing the pico de gallo at the table.

SERVES 4–6

2 lb (1 kg) skirt steak

Juice of 2 limes

1 tablespoon canola oil

1 teaspoon ground cumin

1 teaspoon kosher salt

½ teaspoon freshly ground pepper

2 poblano chiles

10–12 lettuce cups, such as romaine or Bibb lettuce leaves

1 cup (5 oz/155 g) crumbled queso fresco

Fire-Roasted Tomato Salsa (page 22)

Chunky Guacamole or Avocado Crema (page 19)

SKIRT STEAK & ROASTED POBLANO LETTUCE CUP TACOS

CROWD-PLEASER

→>>>>>>>>>

Simple and fast, these tacos make a light but filling meal. The two most important things to remember when cooking skirt steak are always cut across the grain when serving, and make sure you save time for the meat to rest after you cook. For another dinner idea, serve the steak and peppers over the Arroz Blanco (page 117) with cubed avocado.

Build a medium-hot fire in a charcoal grill or preheat a gas grill to medium-high.

Cutting with the grain, cut the steak into 4-inch (10-cm) strips. In a nonreactive bowl, whisk together the lime juice, oil, cumin, salt, and pepper. Add the steak, toss to coat well, and let stand at room temperature for 15 minutes.

When the grill is hot, place the poblanos on the grate directly over the heat and grill, turning with tongs as needed, until blackened all over, about 10 minutes total. Transfer to a bowl and cover with a kitchen towel to cool.

Coat the grill grate lightly with cooking spray. Remove the steak from the marinade. (Discard the marinade.) Arrange the steak on the grate directly over the heat and grill, turning once, until nicely grill-marked and cooked to the desired doneness, about 4 minutes per side for medium-rare. Transfer the steak to a cutting board, cover loosely with aluminum foil, and let rest for about 10 minutes.

Peel the blackened skin from the poblanos (the steam should have loosened them nicely). Core and seed the poblanos and cut into 1-inch (2.5-cm) pieces. Carve the steak across the grain on the diagonal into thin slices.

To assemble, fill the lettuce cups with the steak and poblanos and top each with the queso fresco, dividing them evenly. Serve right away, passing the salsa and guacamole at the table.

SERVES 4–6

2 oz (60 g) achiote paste

2 small chipotle chiles in adobo sauce, minced

½ cup (4 fl oz/125 ml) fresh orange juice
(from 1 or 2 oranges)

¼ cup (2 fl oz/60 ml) canola oil,
plus 1 tablespoon

Kosher salt and freshly ground pepper

2 lb (1 kg) pork loin, cut into ¼-inch (6-mm)
slices

½ pineapple, peeled, cored, and cut
into ½-inch (12-mm) rings

1 red onion, cut into ½-inch (12-mm) slices

12–14 corn or flour tortillas, warmed

¾ cup (6 oz/185 g) Mexican crema or
sour cream (optional)

TACOS AL PASTOR WITH GRILLED PINEAPPLE & ONIONS

Combine the achiote paste, chipotle chiles, orange juice, the ¼ cup oil, and ½ teaspoon salt in a blender and process to a smooth purée. Transfer to a nonreactive bowl, add the pork, and toss to coat thoroughly. Cover and let marinate in the refrigerator for at least 1 hour and up to 4 hours.

Build a medium-hot fire in a charcoal grill or preheat a gas grill to medium-high and set it up for indirect heat: If using a charcoal grill, carefully move the hot coals to one side of the grill. If you are using a gas grill, turn off the middle set of flames when you are ready to grill.

Brush the pineapple and onion on both sides with the 1 tablespoon oil and season with salt and pepper. Arrange the pineapple and onion on the grate directly over the heat and grill, turning once, until soft and nicely grill-marked, about 4 minutes per side. Using tongs, move to the cooler area of the grill and let them continue to soften and caramelize while you cook the pork.

Coat the grill grate lightly with cooking spray. Remove the pork from the marinade. (Discard the marinade.) Arrange the pork on the grate directly over the heat and grill, turning once, until opaque throughout, about 2 minutes per side. Transfer the pork, pineapple, and onion to a cutting board, let cool slightly, and chop into bite-sized pieces.

To assemble, fill the tortillas with pork, pineapple, and onion, dividing them evenly. Dollop with the crema, if using. Serve right away.

SERVES 6

DEEP FLAVORS

The key ingredient in tacos al pastor is the achiote paste, a deep red paste that combines red-hued annatto seed and spices. It's sold in the Latin section of many grocery stores and comes in a block, which will soften when you mix with fresh juice in the blender. Keep any leftover achiote paste in an airtight bag in a dry, cool place.

Mix of ½ cup (4 fl oz/125 ml) low-sodium soy sauce, ¼ cup (2 fl oz/60 ml) sake or water, 3 tablespoons dark sesame oil

6 tablespoons (3 oz/90 g) sugar

1 tablespoon freshly grated ginger

4 cloves garlic, minced

2 tablespoons sesame seeds

1 white onion, cut into large chunks

1 ripe pear, cored and shredded

Kosher salt and freshly ground pepper

1½ lb (750 g) boneless beef short ribs, thinly sliced

2 cups (6 oz/180 g) *each* shredded romaine lettuce and red cabbage

4 radishes, thinly sliced

½ cup (¾ oz/20 g) fresh cilantro, tough stems removed

2 green onions, white and tender green parts only

12–14 flour or corn tortillas, warmed

KOREAN SHORT RIB TACOS WITH CRUNCHY ASIAN SLAW

In a large, nonreactive bowl, stir together the soy mixture, sugar, ginger, garlic, sesame seeds, white onion, pear, 1 teaspoon salt, and 1 teaspoon pepper. Add the thinly sliced beef to the bowl. Using your hands or tongs, toss the meat in the marinade to coat thoroughly. Cover and let marinate in the refrigerator overnight.

When you are ready to grill, remove the beef from the refrigerator and let stand at room temperature for about 15 minutes.

Meanwhile, build a hot fire in a charcoal grill or preheat a gas grill to high. Coat the grill grate lightly with cooking spray. Using tongs, arrange the beef on the grate directly over the heat and grill, turning once, until nicely grill-marked and cooked to the desired doneness, about 2 minutes per side for medium-rare. Using the tongs, transfer the white onion from the bowl to the grate directly over the heat and grill, turning once, until soft, about 5 minutes per side. Transfer to a plate and cover to keep warm. (Discard the marinade.)

To make the crunchy Asian slaw, in a large bowl, toss together the romaine, cabbage, radishes, and cilantro. Chop the green onions coarsely and toss them into the bowl. Add the dressing to the slaw to taste; toss to combine, tasting as you go. Stir half of the Sriracha cream into the slaw. (See recipes at right.)

To assemble, fill the tortillas with the beef, top with a few big pinches of the slaw and some grilled white onion, and serve right away. Pass the extra Sriracha cream at the table for drizzling.

SERVES 6

DRESSING & SAUCE

To make the dressing for the slaw, in a food processor, combine ½ cup (¾ oz/20 g) loosely packed fresh cilantro leaves, 3 green onions, the juice of 2 limes, 2 tablespoons rice vinegar, 1 tablespoon honey, and ½ teaspoon kosher salt. With the machine running, drizzle 2 tablespoons olive oil in a slow, steady stream and process until well blended. To make the Sriracha cream, in a bowl, stir together 1 teaspoon Sriracha and 3 tablespoons sour cream.

½ lb (250 g) thick-cut bacon

1 red onion, halved and cut into ½-inch (12-mm) slices

2 tablespoons olive oil

Kosher salt and freshly ground pepper

3 cups (3 oz/90 g) arugula, stems removed

1 tablespoon fresh lemon juice

8 corn or flour tortillas, warmed

Oaxacan Black Beans (page 104), warmed

BLACK BEAN, BACON & RED ONION TACOS WITH ARUGULA

A BALANCED MEAL

You know the saying: everything is better with bacon! Tacos are no exception. This one is perfect for busy weeknights because it comes together quickly and hits all the high notes for a complete meal: protein from beans and bacon, carbohydrates from tortillas, and a nutritious serving of arugula. For a more fiery version, try this with the Spicy Pinto Beans (page 103) instead.

Heat a large, nonstick frying pan over high heat and add the bacon. Cook, turning once, until crispy, about 8 minutes total. Transfer to a plate lined with paper towels to drain and cool. When cool enough to handle, tear the bacon into bite-sized pieces. Set aside.

Return the frying pan to the stove and heat over high heat. In a small bowl, toss the onion with 1 tablespoon of the olive oil and season well with salt and pepper. Add the onion to the hot pan and sauté, stirring occasionally, until soft and browned all over, about 7 minutes. Remove from the heat and cover to keep warm.

In a large bowl, toss the arugula with the lemon juice and the remaining 1 tablespoon olive oil. Season with salt and pepper.

To assemble, fill the tortillas with the black beans, the bacon, and then the onion. Top with the arugula and serve right away.

SERVES 4

1 can (15 oz/470) black beans,
rinsed and drained

¾ lb (375 g) Spanish chorizo, kielbasa, or other
smoked sausages (optional)

8 large eggs

Kosher salt and freshly ground pepper

2 tablespoons unsalted butter

8 small corn or flour tortillas, warmed

Pico de Gallo (page 20)

¾ cup (3 oz/90 g) shredded Cheddar cheese

1 avocado, pitted, peeled, and sliced

BREAKFAST SOFT TACOS

In a small saucepan over medium heat, warm the black beans, stirring a few times.
Reduce the heat to low to keep the beans warm.

Warm a grill pan or a frying pan to medium-high heat. Cut the chorizo, if using, into
½-inch (12-mm) slices. Coat the pan with nonstick cooking spray and add the chorizo.
Grill, stirring occasionally, until browned on both sides, about 4 minutes total. Turn off
the heat and keep the chorizo warm in the pan.

In a bowl, crack the eggs and beat them with a fork. Season generously with salt and
pepper. Melt the butter in a nonstick frying pan over medium heat. Add the eggs to
the pan and cook, stirring frequently with a rubber spatula, until just set, 4–5 minutes.

To assemble, fill the tortillas with the scrambled eggs, chorizo (if using), black beans,
pico de gallo, Cheddar, and avocado. Serve right away.

SERVES 4

BREAKFAST FOR DINNER

The other name for these popular
tacos is "the emergency dinner"
because breakfast for dinner
always seems to come into play
when there is no time or no
groceries in the house! But this
dinner really has it all and will
please both kids and adults. The
beauty of this recipe is that you
can add whatever you have on
hand: canned beans, sautéed
spinach, leftover sausage, or
even ground beef.

1 tablespoon canola oil, plus more for frying

2 cloves garlic, minced

1 lb (500 g) ground beef

2 teaspoons ground cumin

1 teaspoon kosher salt

1 chipotle chile in adobo sauce, minced (optional)

3 oz (90 g) Monterey jack cheese, shredded

12 flour tortillas (7 inches/18 cm)

Avocado Crema (page 19)

BEEF & MONTEREY JACK TAQUITOS WITH AVOCADO CREMA

LIGHTEN IT UP

>>>>>>>>>

Taquitos form a delicious crispy shell when fried in oil, but you can also lighten them up by baking them instead. For baked taquitos, lightly brush them with canola oil and bake in a 425°F (220°C) oven for about 15 minutes. Make extra taquitos and freeze them; they make a fast microwavable after-school or work snack. Serve these with Watermelon & Feta Salad with Mint & Lime (page 118).

Warm the 1 tablespoon oil in a frying pan over medium-high heat. Add the garlic and sauté just until soft, about 1 minute. Add the ground beef and cook, stirring occasionally and using your spoon to break up any clumps, until the meat is browned and cooked through, about 10 minutes. If there is a lot of fat in the pan, pour off most of it. Add the cumin and salt and cook for 1 minute to toast the cumin. Transfer to a bowl and let cool slightly. Stir in the chipotle chile, if using, and then the Monterey jack.

Pour oil into a frying pan to a depth of about 1½ inches (4 cm); you need enough oil to reach about halfway up the sides of the taquitos. Heat the oil to 350°F (180°C) on a deep-frying or candy thermometer. (If you don't have a thermometer, your best test is to dip the edge of a tortilla into the oil; it should sizzle immediately and vigorously.)

To assemble, lay the tortillas on a clean work surface and fill each with 2 heaping tablespoons of the meat filling. Roll up tightly and secure each with 2 toothpicks (insert the toothpicks just far enough off the seam so you can lay the seam in the hot oil to sear it closed). Working in batches to avoid crowding, add the taquitos to the hot oil, seam side down, and fry until golden brown on the first side, about 1½ minutes. Using tongs, carefully turn and fry on the second side until golden brown, about 1½ minutes longer. As the taquitos are finished, transfer to a plate lined with paper towels to drain and cool.

To serve, remove the toothpicks and arrange on a platter or individual plates. Serve right away with the Avocado Crema.

SERVES 4–6

3 tablespoons olive oil

2 cloves garlic, minced

10 oz (315 g) fresh spinach, tough stems removed

Kosher salt and freshly ground pepper

¾ lb (375 g) Yukon gold potatoes, peeled and cut into ⅛-inch (3-mm) dice

¾ cup (6 fl oz/180 ml) low-sodium chicken broth

1 lb (500 g) Mexican chorizo, casings removed

¾ cup (6 oz/185 g) sour cream

Zest and juice of 1 lime

12–14 corn or flour tortillas, warmed

CHORIZO, POTATO & SPINACH TACOS

Warm 1 tablespoon of the olive oil in a large frying pan over medium-high heat. Add the garlic and sauté just until soft, about 1 minute. Add the spinach, season with salt and pepper, and toss to coat with the oil. Sauté, stirring often, until the spinach is mostly wilted but still holding its shape, about 2 minutes. Transfer to a plate and cover to keep warm.

Return the pan to medium-high heat and warm the remaining 2 tablespoons olive oil. Add the potatoes, season with salt and pepper, and cook, stirring often, until they soften and begin to brown, about 10 minutes. Add the broth and cook until the potatoes absorb the liquid and are tender, 5–7 minutes. Transfer the potatoes to a plate and set aside.

Add the chorizo to the pan and cook, stirring often and using your spoon to break up any clumps, until the meat is browned and cooked through, about 6 minutes. Stir in the potatoes and cook until warmed through, about 2 minutes.

In a small, nonreactive bowl, stir together the sour cream and the lime zest and juice. Season with salt and pepper.

To assemble, fill the tortillas with the spinach and then the chorizo and potato mixture, dividing them evenly. Drizzle with the sour cream sauce and serve right away.

SERVES 4–6

SPICY CHORIZO

Fresh Mexican chorizo—a spicy blend of ground pork sausage, dried chiles, cumin, paprika, and garlic, can be found in the packaged meat section or butcher's counter of grocery stores. Don't confuse it with Spanish chorizo, which is cured. Add color to these tacos with sliced jalapeños and lime wedges for serving, or use yams in place of the potatoes.

1 pork tenderloin, about 1½ lb (750 g)

2 teaspoons canola oil

1 tablespoon Chinese five-spice powder

Kosher salt and freshly ground pepper

3 nectarines, each pitted and cut into 4 wedges

2 teaspoons olive oil

1 tablespoon fresh lime juice

2 teaspoons seeded and minced jalapeño chile

2 tablespoons chopped fresh cilantro

2 tablespoons chopped red onion

10–12 flour or corn tortillas, warmed

¾ cup (6 oz/185 g) sour cream (optional)

CHINESE FIVE-SPICE PORK TACOS WITH NECTARINE SALSA

SPICE IT UP

Chinese five-spice powder is a fragrant combination of cinnamon, cloves, fennel, star anise, and Szechuan peppercorns. It has a perfect mix of sweet and spicy and a little goes a long way. Peaches, plums, and mangoes also work great in this salsa recipe. Serve with Steamed Asparagus with Lemon Butter (page 116).

Build a medium-hot fire in a charcoal grill or preheat a gas grill to medium-high.

Brush the tenderloin with the canola oil. Using your hands, season all over with the Chinese five-spice powder and 1½ teaspoons salt. Let stand at room temperature for about 15 minutes.

Arrange the tenderloin on the grate directly over the heat and grill, turning with tongs every 3 minutes or so, until nicely browned on all sides and an instant-read thermometer inserted into the thickest part registers 140°F (60°C), 12–15 minutes total. Transfer the pork to a cutting board, cover loosely with aluminum foil, and let rest for about 10 minutes. Cut the pork into ¼-inch (6-mm) slices.

While the pork is resting, make the nectarine salsa: Brush the nectarines with the olive oil and season lightly with salt and pepper. Add the nectarines on the grate directly over the heat and grill, using tongs to turn as needed, until soft and nicely grill-marked on all sides, about 4 minutes total. Transfer the nectarines to a cutting board and, when cool enough to handle, and chop into a small dice. Transfer to a bowl and stir in the lime juice, jalapeño, cilantro, and onion. Taste and adjust the seasoning and set aside.

To assemble, fill the tortillas with the pork and spoon the nectarine salsa on top, dividing them evenly. Garnish a dollop of the sour cream, if using. Serve right away.

SERVES 4–6

3 tablespoons canola oil

1 tablespoon ground cumin

1½ teaspoons chili powder

Kosher salt and freshly ground pepper

1½ lb (750 g) boneless, skinless chicken thighs

1 bunch green onions

2 firm-but-ripe mangoes, pitted, peeled, and each cut into 4 thick slices

10–12 flour or corn tortillas, warmed

¼ lb (125 g) Monterey jack cheese, shredded

Chunky Guacamole (page 19)

Lime wedges, for serving

GRILLED CHICKEN, MANGO & GREEN ONION TACOS

Build a medium-hot fire in a charcoal grill or preheat a gas grill to medium-high.

In a large bowl, whisk together 2 tablespoons of the oil, the cumin, chili powder, 1½ teaspoons salt, and ¾ teaspoon pepper. Add the chicken and toss to coat thoroughly. Let stand for 10 minutes at room temperature.

Meanwhile, arrange the green onions and mangoes on a small baking sheet or a large plate. Brush on both sides with the remaining 1 tablespoon oil and season lightly all over with salt and pepper.

Arrange the green onions and mangoes on the grate directly over the heat and grill, turning once, until nicely grill-marked on both sides, about 2 minutes per side for the green onions and 4 minutes per side for the mangoes. Transfer the green onions and mangoes to a cutting board as they are finished. Let cool slightly, then cut the mangoes into 1-inch (2.5-cm) pieces. Transfer the green onions and mangoes to a platter and cover with aluminum foil to keep warm.

Arrange the chicken on the grate directly over the heat and grill, turning once, until nicely grill-marked and opaque throughout, about 4 minutes per side. Transfer to a cutting board and let rest for a few minutes, then cut into 1-inch (2.5-cm) pieces and add to the platter with the green onions and mangoes.

To assemble, fill the tortillas with the chicken, green onions, and mangoes, and serve with Monterey jack and lime wedges. Serve right away, passing the guacamole at the table.

SERVES 4–6

THE PERFECT MANGO

Sweet and fragrant, mangoes are even better when grilled. As their sugars caramelize, they become more luscious and juicy. A few things to note about choosing a mango: you can tell if a mango is ripe if it smells like fresh mango and is slightly soft when you squeeze it. Like an avocado, mangoes continue to ripen after they are picked, so make sure you buy them ahead of time.

1½ tablespoons ancho chile powder

1½ tablespoons ground cumin

Kosher salt and freshly ground pepper

3 tablespoons canola oil

1½ lb (750 g) boneless, skinless chicken thighs

3 ears of corn, husks and silks removed

¾ cup (4½ oz/140 g) cherry tomatoes, quartered

2 firm-but-ripe avocados, pitted, peeled, and cut into small cubes

1 tablespoon olive oil

3 tablespoons chopped fresh cilantro

8 corn or flour tortillas, warmed

ANCHO CHILE CHICKEN TACOS WITH CORN-AVOCADO SALSA

VERSATILE FLAVOR

This corn and avocado salsa makes a fantastic topping for a number of different tacos. Any leftover chicken works well tucked into a quesadilla for lunch the next day. When selecting ancho chile powder, keep in mind that different varieties vary in spiciness, so select one that suits your preference.

In a bowl, whisk together the chile powder, cumin, 1½ teaspoons salt, and 2 tablespoons of the canola oil. Add the chicken and toss to coat thoroughly. Cover and let marinate in the refrigerator for about 1 hour.

Warm the remaining 1 tablespoon canola oil in a frying pan over medium-high heat. Add the chicken. (Discard the marinade.) Cook the chicken, turning once, until lightly browned and opaque throughout, about 5 minutes per side. Transfer to a cutting board and let rest for a few minutes, then cut into ½-inch (12-mm) pieces. Cover loosely with aluminum foil to keep warm.

To make the salsa, bring a large pot of lightly salted water to a rapid boil. Add the corn and cook until fork-tender, about 8 minutes. Drain and let cool. When cool enough to handle, cut the kernels from the cobs and transfer to a large bowl. Toss with the tomatoes, avocados, olive oil, and cilantro. Season with salt and pepper.

To assemble, fill the tortillas with the chicken and top with the corn salsa, dividing them evenly. Serve right away.

SERVES 4

3 cloves garlic, unpeeled

2 chipotle chiles in adobo sauce

1 can (14½ oz/455 g) diced fire-roasted tomatoes

2 tablespoons olive oil

1 white onion, halved and cut into ½-inch (12-mm) slices

Kosher salt and freshly ground pepper

1 teaspoon dried Mexican oregano

2½ lb (1.25 kg) bone-in, skinless chicken thighs

12–14 corn or flour tortillas, warmed

1 cup (5 oz/155 g) crumbled queso fresco

2 avocados, pitted, peeled, and cut into ½-inch (12-mm) cubes

CHICKEN TINGA TACOS

Put the garlic in a dry frying pan over high heat and cook, turning a few times, until blackened in some spots on all sides, 3–4 minutes. Set aside and let cool. When cool enough to handle, peel the cloves. Combine the garlic, chipotle chiles, and tomatoes in a blender and process to a coarse (but not chunky) purée.

Warm the olive oil in a heavy-bottomed frying pan over medium-high heat. Add the onion, season with salt and pepper, and cook, stirring often, until the onion is lightly browned, about 8 minutes. Stir in the oregano and the chipotle sauce and bring to a boil. Nestle the chicken into the sauce, cover, and cook until the chicken is opaque throughout, 25–30 minutes. Remove from the heat and set aside.

Using tongs, transfer the chicken to a plate and let cool. When cool enough to handle, using your hands or 2 forks, pull the meat from the bones and shred into bite-sized pieces. Return the chicken to the sauce and rewarm everything gently over medium-low heat, about 4 minutes. Season with salt and pepper.

To assemble, fill the tortillas with the chicken tinga and top with the queso fresco and avocados, dividing them evenly. Serve right away.

SERVES 6

MAKE IT AHEAD

This is the perfect party dish for a crowd because it can be made a couple of days ahead. The flavors only get better with time. To serve, put out a warmed dish of chicken tinga and let guests assemble their tacos, garnishing with cheese and avocados. Serve with Butter Lettuce, Papaya & Avocado Salad (page 112) and a plate piled high with brownies for a complete meal to entertain.

½ cup (4 fl oz/125 ml) good-quality tequila

½ cup (4 fl oz/125 ml) fresh orange juice
(from 1 or 2 oranges)

⅓ cup (3 fl oz/80 ml) fresh lime juice
(from about 3 limes), plus 1 tablespoon

2 tablespoons olive oil, plus 2 teaspoons

1½ teaspoons chili powder

Kosher salt and freshly ground pepper

2 lb (1 kg) boneless, skinless chicken breasts

4 watermelon, French, or plain red radishes,
halved and thinly sliced

2 firm-but-ripe avocados, pitted, peeled,
and cut into ½-inch (12-mm) cubes

10–12 flour or corn tortillas, warmed

TEQUILA-LIME CHICKEN TACOS WITH RADISH-AVOCADO SALAD

ALFRESCO FAVORITE

>>>>>>>>>

Serve this refreshing dish with Corn on the Cob Three Ways (page 106) and sliced watermelon for a tasty summer meal. The longer you can marinate the chicken, the better the flavors will be after you grill. Visually stunning, watermelon radishes are in season in spring and fall. If you can't find them, substitute French or regular radishes, which taste almost exactly the same.

In a large, nonreactive bowl, whisk together the tequila, orange juice, the ⅓ cup lime juice, the 2 tablespoons olive oil, the chili powder, and 1 teaspoon salt. Add the chicken and toss to coat thoroughly. Cover and let marinate in the refrigerator for at least 3 hours and up to overnight.

Build a medium-hot fire in a charcoal grill or preheat a gas grill to medium-high.

Remove the chicken from the marinade. (Discard the marinade.) Arrange the chicken on the grate directly over the heat and grill, turning once, until nicely grill-marked and opaque throughout, about 6 minutes per side. Transfer the chicken to a cutting board, cover loosely with aluminum foil, and let rest for about 10 minutes. Cut the chicken into ½-inch (12-mm) pieces.

Meanwhile, make the radish-avocado salad: In a nonreactive bowl, toss together the radish slices and avocado cubes. Gently stir in the 1 tablespoon lime juice and the 2 teaspoons olive oil and season with salt and pepper.

To assemble, fill the tortillas with the chicken and top with the radish-avocado salad. Serve right away.

SERVES 4–6

1 tablespoon olive oil

2 lb (1 kg) ground turkey

1½ tablespoons chili powder

Kosher salt and freshly ground pepper

1 small chipotle chile in adobo sauce, minced (or use ½ if you want mild spiciness)

¾ cup (6 fl oz/180 ml) low-sodium chicken broth

⅓ cup (½ oz/15 g) loosely packed fresh cilantro leaves, chopped

Crispy Taco Shells (page 23)

Refried Beans (page 105), warmed

3 oz (90 g) Monterey jack cheese, shredded

Pico de Gallo (page 20) or Salsa Verde (page 27)

CHIPOTLE TURKEY TACOS WITH REFRIED BEANS

WEEKNIGHT STAPLE

These tacos come together in minutes, especially if you prepare the turkey filling a day in advance. In a time crunch, purchase crispy shells and refried beans. The addition of a chipotle chile kicks up the flavor a notch. If you are looking for a recipe for a more traditional turkey taco, substitute the chipotle for 1 tablespoon tomato paste.

Warm the olive oil in a nonstick frying pan over medium-high heat. Add the ground turkey and cook, stirring occasionally and using your spoon to break up any clumps, until the meat is browned and cooked through, about 6 minutes.

Stir in the chili powder, 1½ teaspoons salt, the chipotle chile (to taste), and the broth. Bring to a simmer, reduce the heat to low, and cook gently, stirring occasionally, until the sauce thickens, about 5 minutes. Remove from the heat and stir in the cilantro. Taste and adjust the seasoning with salt and pepper.

To assemble, fill the crispy shells in this order: beans, turkey mixture, and Monterey jack. Serve right away, passing the salsa at the table.

SERVES 4–6

⅓ cup (½ oz/15 g) loosely packed fresh cilantro leaves, chopped

2 tablespoons fresh lime juice

2 cloves garlic, minced

1 teaspoon *each* chili powder and ground cumin

½ teaspoon onion powder

Kosher salt and freshly ground pepper

4 tablespoons (2 fl oz/60 ml) canola oil

1½ lb (750 g) boneless, skinless chicken breasts, cut into ½-inch (12-mm) strips

1 *each* red and yellow bell pepper, seeded and cut into ½-inch (12-mm) strips

1 yellow onion, halved and cut into ½-inch (12-mm) strips

10 corn or flour tortillas, warmed

¼ lb (125 g) Monterey jack cheese, shredded

CHICKEN & BELL PEPPER FAJITAS

In a large nonreactive bowl, whisk together the cilantro, lime juice, garlic, chili powder, cumin, onion powder, ½ teaspoon salt, and 3 tablespoons of the oil. Add the chicken to the bowl and toss to coat well. Cover and let marinate in the refrigerator for at least 1 hour and up to overnight.

Warm a large grill pan or a cast-iron frying pan over high heat. In a medium bowl, toss the bell peppers and onion with the remaining 1 tablespoon oil and season well with salt and pepper. Add the vegetables to the hot pan and grill until soft and lightly browned, 6–8 minutes. Transfer to a large plate.

Reduce the heat to medium-high. Working in batches as needed to avoid crowding, add the chicken to the pan and cook, turning or stirring occasionally, until grill-marked and opaque throughout, about 10 minutes. If working in batches, transfer each batch as it is finished to the plate with the vegetables. When all of the chicken is cooked, return all of the chicken and the vegetables to the pan, along with any juices accumulated on the plate, and cook just until everything is warmed through, about 3 minutes.

To assemble, fill the tortillas with the chicken and vegetables. Serve right away, passing the Monterey jack at the table.

SERVES 4

SIMPLE SOLUTIONS

◄◄◄◄◄◄◄◄

Fajitas are a great weeknight dinner to make ahead so that when it's time to sit down for dinner, you can simply reheat the filling and load up the tortillas. You can use this recipe to make any number of fajitas: beef, shrimp, tofu, or even all veggies. (Any leftover filling makes a fantastic meal in a thermos topped with salsa and tortilla chips on the side.) Serve with Avocado Crema (page 19) and Pico de Gallo (page 20).

Kosher salt and freshly ground pepper

1½ lb (750 g) boneless, skinless chicken thighs

1 tablespoon canola oil

2 teaspoons ground cumin

2 teaspoons chili powder

2 ears of corn, husks and silks removed

Avocado dressing (see sidebar)

10 cups (10 oz/315 g) chopped romaine lettuce

4 ripe plum (Roma) tomatoes, chopped

1 can (15 oz/470 g) black beans, rinsed and drained

2 oz (60 g) Monterey jack cheese, shredded

20 corn tortilla chips

GRILLED CHICKEN TACO SALAD WITH AVOCADO DRESSING

Build a medium-hot fire in a charcoal grill or preheat a gas grill to medium-high. At the same time, bring a large pot of lightly salted water to a boil over high heat.

Arrange the chicken on a large plate. Brush on both sides with the canola oil and season all over with the cumin, chili powder, and 1 teaspoon salt. Coat the grill grate lightly with cooking spray. Arrange the chicken on the grate directly over the heat and grill, turning once, until nicely grill-marked and opaque throughout, about 4 minutes per side. Transfer to a cutting board, cover loosely with aluminum foil, and let rest while you cook the corn and make the dressing. Cover the grill to keep the coals warm.

Add the corn to the boiling water and cook until fork-tender, about 4 minutes. Drain the corn well, arrange on the grate directly over the heat and grill, turning as needed, until blackened in spots all over, about 6 minutes total. Transfer to a cutting board and let cool.

When the corn is cool enough to handle, cut the kernels from the cobs. Cut the chicken into 1-inch (2.5-cm) pieces. In a large bowl, toss the lettuce with just enough dressing to coat thoroughly and divide among 4 bowls. Top each salad with chicken, corn, tomatoes, black beans, and Monterey jack, dividing them evenly. Crumble the tortilla chips over the top of each salad. Serve right away, passing any extra dressing at the table.

SERVES 4

AVOCADO DRESSING

To make the dressing, scoop the flesh from 1 pitted avocado into a blender. Add 1 clove garlic, ¼ cup (⅓ oz/10 g) loosely packed fresh cilantro leaves, ¼ cup (2 fl oz/60 ml) buttermilk, 2 tablespoons sour cream or plain yogurt, 2 tablespoons red wine vinegar, and 2 tablespoons olive oil and process to a smooth purée. Season with salt and pepper.

1¼ lb (625 g) boneless, skinless chicken breasts

2 teaspoons canola oil

2 teaspoons ground cumin

2 teaspoons chili powder

½ teaspoon kosher salt

6 oz (185 g) corn tortilla chips

Oaxacan Black Beans (page 104)

6 oz (185 g) Monterey jack cheese, shredded

2 ripe tomatoes, diced

1 ripe avocado, pitted, peeled, and cut into ½-inch (12-mm) cubes

Pickled Jalapeños & Carrots (page 30) (optional)

½ cup (4 oz/125 g) sour cream

CHICKEN TACO NACHOS

NACHO NIGHT

>>>>>>>>>

Everyone gets excited about nachos for dinner! Loaded with calcium from the cheese, protein from the chicken and the beans, and topped with chunks of fresh tomatoes and avocado, nachos are both satisfying and nutritious. Serve with Chipotle & Maple-Roasted Sweet Potatoes (page 115) to round out the meal.

Preheat the oven to 375°F (190°C). Line a baking sheet with aluminum foil.

Arrange the chicken on a large plate. Brush on both sides with the canola oil and season all over with the cumin, chili powder, and salt. Arrange on the prepared pan and bake until opaque throughout, about 25 minutes. Remove from the oven and let cool. When cool enough to handle, using your hands or 2 forks, shred the meat into bite-sized pieces.

Preheat the broiler.

Spread the tortilla chips in a single layer in a large cast-iron pan or on a clean baking sheet. Top with the black beans, then the chicken, and then the Monterey jack. Slip under the broiler and broil just until the Monterey jack is melted, about 3 minutes.

Remove the nachos from the broiler and, using a large, wide spatula, carefully transfer to a serving platter. Garnish with the tomatoes, avocado, and pickled vegetables, if using. Dollop with the sour cream and serve right away.

SERVES 4

1 lb (500 g) medium shrimp, peeled and deveined

1 tablespoon canola oil

2 teaspoons chili powder

1 teaspoon kosher salt

8 flour or corn tortillas, warmed

Creamy Cilantro Slaw (page 26)

Pico de Gallo (page 20)

CHILI-RUBBED SHRIMP TACOS WITH CREAMY CILANTRO SLAW

In a bowl, toss the shrimp with the canola oil, chili powder, and salt. Set aside.

Warm a grill pan or a nonstick frying pan over high heat. When the pan is very hot, add the shrimp and grill or sear, turning once, until bright pink and opaque throughout, about 2 minutes per side. Transfer the shrimp to a plate.

To assemble, fill the tortillas with the shrimp, dividing them evenly. Pile a few big pinches or a scoop of the creamy cilantro slaw on each and serve right away, passing the pico de gallo at the table.

SERVES 4

SHRIMP LOGIC

Most shrimp from the seafood counter of a grocery store have been frozen at some point, so consider buying a bag of frozen shrimp from the freezer aisle; it's not only more economical but also convenient. You can use the amount you need and keep the rest frozen for another dinner. Medium shrimp are the perfect size for tacos.

1 cup (5 oz/155 g) all-purpose flour

Kosher salt and freshly ground pepper

1 cup (8 fl oz/250 ml) dark Mexican beer

1 lb (500 g) cod fillets

Canola oil for frying

8 corn or flour tortillas, warmed

Tangy Coleslaw (page 26)

Taqueria Guacamole (page 19)

Fire-Roasted Tomato Salsa (page 22)

BAJA-STYLE BEER-BATTERED FISH TACOS

CLASSIC CROWD-PLEASER

Piled high with crunchy, creamy, and fiery toppings, these fried fish tacos will earn a spot in any fish taco enthusiast's heart. Choose a beer for the batter that you will also enjoy sipping alongside the tacos. To avoid soggy fish, cook it in a small saucepan: it uses less oil and it's easier to maintain the heat.

In a large bowl, whisk together the flour, 2 teaspoons salt, and ½ teaspoon pepper. Slowly whisk in the beer and stir until there are no lumps left. Let the batter rest for 10 minutes.

Cut the cod into 2-inch (5-cm) pieces and season well with salt and pepper. Drop the fish into the batter and stir to coat. Using a slotted spoon, remove the fish from the batter, letting the excess batter drip back into the bowl, and transfer to a plate.

Preheat the oven to 200°F (95°C).

Pour oil into a small, heavy-bottomed saucepan to a depth of 1 inch (2.5 cm) and heat to 350°F (180°C) on a deep-frying or candy thermometer. (If you don't have a thermometer, your best test is to dip the corner of a piece of fish into the oil; it should sizzle immediately and vigorously.)

Carefully add a few pieces of the fish at a time to the hot oil, being careful not to crowd the pan. Cook, turning once, until the batter is golden brown all over, about 3 minutes total. Using tongs, transfer the fish to a baking sheet lined with paper towels to drain, and place in the oven to keep warm. Repeat to fry the remaining fish.

To serve, set out a platter of the fish along with the tortillas, coleslaw, guacamole, and salsa and let everyone create their own tacos.

SERVES 4

2 tablespoons all-purpose flour

1½ tablespoons chili powder

1 tablespoon dark brown sugar

1 teaspoon *each* onion powder, garlic powder, and smoked paprika

Kosher salt and freshly ground pepper

2 lb (1 kg) center-cut salmon fillet, pin bones and skin removed

3 tablespoons olive oil

2 tablespoons sherry vinegar

½ teaspoon Dijon mustard

¼ small green savoy cabbage, shredded (about 2 cups/6 oz/185 g)

8–12 flour or corn tortillas, warmed

Pineapple-Jicama Salsa (page 29)

BLACKENED SALMON TACOS WITH SPICY CABBAGE

In a small bowl, stir together the flour, chili powder, brown sugar, onion powder, garlic powder, smoked paprika, and ½ teaspoon salt. Pat the salmon dry with a paper towel, then coat on all sides with the spice rub.

Heat 2 tablespoons of the olive oil in a nonstick frying pan over high heat. Add the salmon to the hot oil and cook, turning once, for about 5 minutes per side for rare. Transfer to a cutting board, cover loosely with aluminum foil, and let rest for about 10 minutes.

Meanwhile, make the spicy cabbage: In the bottom of a large bowl, stir together the vinegar and mustard and season with salt and pepper. Whisk in the remaining 1 tablespoon olive oil until well blended. Add the cabbage and toss to coat thoroughly with the dressing. Taste and adjust the seasoning.

Transfer the salmon to a platter and, using a fork, flake the salmon into large chunks. To serve, set out the platter of salmon along with the tortillas, salsa, and cabbage and let everyone create their own tacos.

SERVES 4–6

FISH-COOKING TIPS

Spice-crusted salmon gets crisp on the outside and stays moist and tender on the inside when seared in a hot pan. Be sure not to move it in the pan for at least 5 minutes to get a nice sear. To make this into a taco bowl, serve the spicy cabbage, flaked salmon, and salsa atop a bed of brown or white rice.

1 clove garlic

Kosher salt and freshly ground pepper

1 large egg plus 1 large egg yolk

1 cup (8 fl oz/250 ml) canola oil

Zest and juice of 1 Meyer lemon

1 tablespoon finely chopped fresh cilantro

½ small red cabbage, shredded
(about 3 cups/9 oz/280 g)

2 tablespoons rice wine vinegar

4 tablespoons (2 fl oz/60 ml) olive oil

16 medium scallops, debearded

8 small flour or corn tortillas, warmed

PAN-SEARED SCALLOPS WITH MEYER LEMON–CILANTRO AIOLI

DINNER IN A JIFFY

→≫≫≫≫≫≫≫

Sweet, tender scallops cook very fast, about 2 minutes per side in a searingly hot pan. To get them golden brown, be sure to dry them well with a paper towel before you season them. Tucked into tortillas with crunchy cabbage and lemony aioli, these scrumptious tacos are worthy of company.

To make the aioli, put the garlic and a big pinch of salt in a food processor and pulse several times until the garlic is finely chopped. Add the whole egg and the egg yolk and process until well blended. With the machine running, drizzle in a few drops of the canola oil, followed by the remaining oil in a slow, steady stream until it is completely incorporated and emulsified. Transfer the aioli to a bowl and stir in the lemon zest and juice and the cilantro. Season with salt and set aside at room temperature until ready to serve.

In a large bowl, toss the cabbage with the vinegar and 2 tablespoons of the olive oil. Season with salt and pepper and let stand at room temperature to allow the flavors to blend.

Warm the remaining 2 tablespoons olive oil in a frying pan over high heat. Season both sides of the scallops with salt and pepper. (If your scallops are very large, you may want to cut them in half horizontally through the thickness.) Add the scallops to the hot oil and sear, turning once, just until opaque throughout, 2–3 minutes per side. Remove from the heat.

To assemble, fill each tortilla with 2 scallops or 4 scallop halves and top with a handful of the cabbage and a generous drizzle of the aioli. Serve right away.

SERVES 4

1 cup (1 oz/30 g) loosely packed fresh cilantro, tough stems removed

½ cup (¾ oz/20 g) loosely packed fresh flat-leaf parsley, tough stems removed

2 cloves garlic

1 small jalapeño chile, seeded and chopped

1 teaspoon ground cumin

Kosher salt and freshly ground pepper

½ cup (4 fl oz/125 ml) olive oil, plus 3 tablespoons

2 whole red snappers, about 1½ lb (750 g) each, scaled and cleaned

1 lemon, cut into 6–8 slices

8–12 flour or corn tortillas, warmed

GRILLED RED SNAPPER TACOS WITH MEXICAN CHIMICHURRI

FIT FOR A PARTY

>>>>>>>>>>

Grilling a whole fish makes a stunning presentation, great for entertaining. But it's also simple enough to serve as a weeknight dinner. Have your fish monger prepare the fish by cleaning (gutting) and scaling it. Don't make the chimichurri sauce too far in advance as it starts to lose its beautiful green color after a few hours.

Build a hot fire in a charcoal grill or preheat a gas grill to high.

To make the chimichurri, combine the cilantro, parsley, garlic, jalapeño, cumin, and ½ teaspoon salt in a food processor and pulse until finely chopped, scraping down the sides with a spatula as needed. With the machine running, drizzle in the ½ cup olive oil in a slow, steady stream and process until well combined. Taste and adjust the seasoning with salt. Transfer to a bowl and set aside.

Brush both sides of the fish with the 3 tablespoons olive oil and season generously with salt and pepper. Stuff the belly of each fish with 3 or 4 lemon slices. If you have a fish basket, place your fish inside and then onto the grill. If you don't have a fish basket, coat the grill grate generously with cooking spray and arrange the fish on the grate directly over the heat (use a large, flat spatula in one hand and an oven mitt in the other when flipping the fish). Cover and grill the fish for 10 minutes. Turn the fish, re-cover the grill, and grill until the flesh of the fish is opaque throughout and flakes easily with a fork, about 10 minutes more.

To serve, transfer the fish to a platter and drizzle with a few tablespoons of the chimichurri. Using a fork, flake off pieces of the fish and fill the tortillas with fish, adding more chimichurri as desire. Serve right away.

SERVES 4–6

---

3 tablespoons canola oil

1 dried New Mexico chile, seeded and ground or finely chopped (depending on spice preference)

2 cloves garlic, minced

2 teaspoons ground cumin

1 teaspoon kosher salt

2 lb (1 kg) halibut fillets

1 bay leaf, torn in half

8–12 corn or flour tortillas, warmed

Creamy Cilantro Slaw (page 26)

Pico de Gallo (page 20)

GRILLED HALIBUT TACOS

YEAR-ROUND "GRILLING"

→→→→→→→

Grilled fish tacos always seem like a special treat, but really they couldn't be simpler to make. Halibut can be expensive, so try other firm white fish such as cod or tilapia. If you want to make fish tacos during the winter, simply follow this recipe and cook the fish in a hot stovetop grill pan. During the winter, you can cook the fish under the broiler.

In a small bowl, stir together the canola oil, chile, garlic, cumin, and salt. Place the fish in a nonreactive dish and rub the marinade all over both sides. Place the bay leaf on top of the fish. Cover and refrigerate for 1 hour.

Build a medium-hot fire in a charcoal grill or preheat a gas grill to medium-high. Remove the fish from the refrigerator and let stand at room temperature for 15 minutes.

Coat the grill grate lightly with cooking spray. Arrange the fillets on the grate directly over the heat, flesh side down. Cover the grill and cook for 5 minutes. Using a large, wide spatula, carefully turn the fish, then close the lid again. Grill until opaque throughout but still very moist, about 5 minutes longer. Transfer the fish to a serving platter and, using a fork, flake the fish into large chunks.

To serve, set out the platter of fish along with the tortillas, coleslaw, and pico de gallo and let everyone create their own tacos.

SERVES 4–6

WHAT YOU NEED

½ cup (4 oz/125 g) sour cream

2 tablespoons heavy cream

1½ teaspoons prepared wasabi paste

1 tablespoon fresh lemon juice

1 teaspoon low-sodium soy sauce

Kosher salt and freshly ground pepper

1 cup (3 oz/90 g) *each* shredded green and red cabbage

4 teaspoons seasoned rice wine vinegar

1 teaspoon mirin

2 tablespoons olive oil

1 lb (500 g) tuna steak, cut into 4 equal rectangular pieces

1 avocado, pitted, peeled, and thinly sliced

8 corn or flour tortillas, warmed

TUNA TACOS WITH AVOCADO & WASABI CREMA

To make the wasabi crema, in a bowl, stir together the sour cream, heavy cream, wasabi paste, lemon juice, soy sauce, and ¼ teaspoon salt. Let stand at room temperature to allow the flavors to blend until you are ready to serve.

In a large bowl, toss together the cabbages. Add the vinegar, mirin, 1 tablespoon of the olive oil, and salt and pepper to taste and toss to mix well. Set aside.

Heat the remaining 1 tablespoon olive oil in a nonstick frying pan over high heat. Add the tuna to the hot oil and sear, turning once, until nicely browned on both sides, about 2 minutes per side for medium-rare. Transfer to a cutting board and let rest for a few minutes, then slice thinly.

To assemble, fill the tortillas with the tuna, dividing it evenly, and top with a handful of the cabbage, some avocado slices, and a generous drizzle of the wasabi crema. Serve right away.

SERVES 4

JAPANESE-MEXICAN HYBRID

These delicious tuna tacos combine flavors from Japanese and Mexican cuisines. It's best to buy fish fresh the same day you plan to cook it. When searing fish, make sure your pan is extremely hot but not smoking; for maximum flavor and tenderness, first dry the fish with paper towel then season generously before adding it to the pan.

Canola oil for frying

8 corn tortillas (5 inches/13 cm)

Kosher salt

24 medium shrimp, peeled and deveined

1 tablespoon chili powder

2 teaspoons ground cumin

Taqueria Guacamole (page 19)

Spicy Pinto Beans (page 103), warmed

½ cup (2½ oz/75 g) crumbled queso fresco

Fire-Roasted Tomato Salsa (page 22)

¼ cup (⅓ oz/10 g) loosely packed fresh cilantro leaves (optional)

SHRIMP TOSTADAS WITH BEANS & GUACAMOLE

Pour oil into a small frying pan over medium-high heat to a depth of ½ inch (12 mm) and heat to 350°F (180°C) on a deep-frying or candy thermometer. (If you don't have a thermometer, your best test is to dip the edge of a tortilla into the oil; it should sizzle immediately and vigorously.)

Using tongs, add the tortillas, 1 at a time, to the hot oil and fry, turning once, until crispy, about 1 minute per side. Transfer to a plate lined with paper towels to drain. Sprinkle with salt while the tortillas are still warm.

Warm a grill pan or a cast-iron frying pan over high heat. In a bowl, toss the shrimp with 1 tablespoon oil, the chili powder, and cumin. Season with salt and add to the hot pan. Grill or sear, turning once, until the shrimp are bright pink and opaque throughout, about 2 minutes per side. Transfer to a plate and set aside.

To assemble the tostadas, put 2 tortillas on each of 4 individual plates and layer on the toppings in this order: guacamole, pinto beans, shrimp, queso fresco, and salsa. Garnish with the cilantro leaves, if using, and serve right away.

SERVES 4

FLAT TACO TREAT

A tostada is a flat crispy tortilla piled high with flavorful fillings that is easy to make at home. If you are short on time, you can find crispy tortillas at most supermarkets near the tortillas. For a great party snack, make mini tostadas by using small round tortilla chips. This recipe is also delicious with chicken or flank steak.

WHAT YOU NEED

2 tablespoons olive oil

1 red onion, halved and cut into ¼-inch (6-mm) slices

Kosher salt and freshly ground pepper

2 cloves garlic, minced

10 oz (315 g) baby kale or stemmed (including tough center spines) and chopped regular kale

1 can (15 oz/470 g) pinto beans, rinsed and drained

⅓ cup (3 fl oz/80 ml) low-sodium vegetable or chicken broth

Juice of 1 lime

8 multigrain, corn, or flour tortillas, warmed

¾ cup (4 oz/125 g) crumbled cotija cheese

¼ cup (⅓ oz/10 g) loosely packed fresh cilantro leaves

¾ cup (6 oz/185 g) Mexican crema or sour cream (optional)

BEANS & GREENS TACOS

Warm the olive oil in a large frying pan over medium-high heat. Add the onion and season with salt and pepper. Cook, stirring often, until translucent, about 15 minutes. Add the garlic and sauté just until soft, about 1 minute.

Add the kale and toss several times to coat with the oil. Add the beans and broth and cook, stirring often, until the kale is wilted and the beans are warmed through, about 4 minutes. Stir in the lime juice and season with salt and pepper.

To assemble, fill the tortillas with the beans and greens mixture. Top with the cotija and cilantro. Serve right away, passing the crema at the table, if using.

SERVES 4

POWER MEAL

◄◄◄◄◄◄◄◄◄——

These ultranutritious tacos are loaded with protein- and fiber-rich beans and superfood kale. You can add more heft to this dish by topping each taco with a generous dollop of Taqueria Guacamole (page 19). Leftover beans and greens are delicious topped with a fried egg for breakfast or dinner the next day.

1 butternut squash, about 2 lb (1 kg), peeled, seeded, and cut into ¾-inch (2-cm) cubes

3 tablespoons olive oil

1 tablespoon chili powder

Kosher salt and freshly ground pepper

1 cup (8 oz/250 g) sour cream or crème fraîche

1 small chipotle chile in adobo sauce, minced

1 teaspoon fresh lime juice

10 oz (315 g) baby spinach or stemmed and chopped regular spinach

8–10 flour or corn tortillas, warmed

Oaxacan Black Beans (page 104), warmed

ROASTED BUTTERNUT SQUASH, SPINACH & BLACK BEAN TACOS

SWEET & SPICY

→→→→→→→→

Roasting butternut squash brings out its natural sweetness, which balances nicely with the earthiness of the spinach and beans, and the spiciness of the chipotle crema. You can adjust the amount of chipotle pepper you add depending on how spicy you want this. Extra chipotle crema is delicious drizzled over nachos or breakfast tacos, or as a dip for slices of cucumber and jicama.

Preheat the oven to 400°F (200°C). Line a baking sheet with parchment paper.

Pile the squash on the prepared baking sheet, drizzle with 2 tablespoons of the olive oil, and sprinkle with the chili powder and 1 teaspoon salt and toss to coat. Spread the squash in a single layer and roast, stirring once about halfway through, until very soft and browned around the edges, about 25 minutes. Remove from the oven and set aside.

While the squash is roasting, make the chipotle crema: In a small bowl, stir together the sour cream, chipotle, and lime juice. Season with salt and set aside at room temperature until ready to serve.

Warm the remaining 1 tablespoon olive oil in a frying pan over medium-high heat. Add the spinach, season with salt and pepper, and cook, stirring often, until just barely wilted, about 3 minutes.

To assemble, fill the tortillas with the squash, spinach, and beans. Drizzle generously with the chipotle crema and serve right away.

SERVES 4

3 tablespoons olive oil

2 teaspoons chili powder

1 teaspoon kosher salt

4 ears of corn, husks and silks removed

3 zucchini, cut lengthwise
into ¼-inch (6-mm) slices

8–10 corn or flour tortillas, warmed

¾ cup (4 oz/125 g) crumbled cotija cheese

¼ cup (⅓ oz/10 g) loosely packed fresh
cilantro leaves

GRILLED CORN & ZUCCHINI TACOS

Build a medium-hot fire in a charcoal grill or preheat a gas grill to medium-high.

In a small bowl, stir together the olive oil, chili powder, and salt. Brush the corn and
zucchini all over with the chili oil.

Arrange the zucchini on the grate directly over the heat and grill, turning once, until
nicely grill-marked and fork-tender, about 3 minutes per side. Transfer to a cutting board.
Arrange the corn on the grate directly over the heat and grill, rotating every couple of
minutes, until blackened in spots all over, about 8 minutes total. Transfer the corn to
the cutting board.

Cut the zucchini into ½-inch (12-mm) pieces and transfer to a bowl. When the corn is
cool enough to handle, cut the kernels from the cobs and transfer to a bowl.

To assemble, fill the tortillas with the corn and zucchini. Top with the cotija and
cilantro and serve right away.

SERVES 4

SUMMERTIME FAVORITE

Wait to make these tacos in the
summer, when fresh corn is
sweet and zucchini are plentiful.
In the winter, you can make a
version with defrosted frozen corn
kernels and winter squash. The
ingredients cook in mere minutes
on the grill, making this a simple
and quick weeknight meal. Serve
with Pickled Red Onions (page 30)
and lime wedges.

5 tablespoons (3 fl oz/80 ml) canola oil

½ teaspoon chili powder

1¼ teaspoon smoked paprika

5 portobello mushrooms, stemmed and brushed clean

4 serrano chiles

2 small red onions, cut into ½-inch (12-mm) slices

Kosher salt

1 cup (8 oz/250 g) sour cream or crème fraîche

2 teaspoons fresh lemon juice

8–10 flour or corn tortillas, warmed

GRILLED PORTOBELLO & CHILE TACOS WITH SMOKED CREMA

EARTHY, SMOKY FARE

>>>>>>>>>

Here, grilled portobello mushrooms get a lift from being tucked into warm tortillas with charred and smoky serrano chiles and sweet onions. Cooling crema, flavored with a hint of smoked paprika and lime, is the ideal garnish. Try this with other seasonal vegetables such as sliced eggplant or zucchini, or a mixture of mushrooms.

Build a medium-hot fire in a charcoal grill or preheat a gas grill to medium-high. Coat the grill grate lightly with cooking spray.

In a small bowl, stir together the oil, chili powder, and ½ teaspoon of the smoked paprika. Brush the mushrooms, serranos, and onion on all sides with the chili oil and season generously with salt.

Arrange the vegetables on the grate directly over the heat and grill, turning as needed, until nicely grill-marked and tender, about 4 minutes per side for the mushrooms and serranos and 6 minutes per side for the onions. Transfer the vegetables to a cutting board. Cut the mushrooms and onions into 1-inch (2.5-cm) pieces. Stem and cut the serranos in half lengthwise.

To make the smoked paprika crema, in a bowl, stir together the sour cream, lemon juice, the remaining ¾ teaspoon smoked paprika, and ¼ teaspoon salt. Set the crema aside at room temperature until ready to serve.

To assemble, fill the tortillas with the mushrooms and onions and drizzle generously with the crema. Pass the serranos at the table so that guests can add heat as they like. Serve right away.

SERVES 4

3 sweet potatoes, about 1½ lb (750 g) total, peeled and cut into ¼-inch (6-mm) dice

3 tablespoons canola oil

2 teaspoons ground cumin

2 teaspoons chili powder

1 teaspoon ground coriander

1 teaspoon kosher salt

1 can (4 oz/125 g) chopped fire-roasted green chiles

8–10 corn or flour tortillas, warmed

¼ lb (125 g) Monterey jack cheese, shredded

Avocado Crema (page 19)

SPICED SWEET POTATO, GREEN CHILE & MONTEREY JACK TACOS

ADAPTABLE TACO

While delicious enclosed in a warm tortilla, the filling for this taco also works well in a quesadilla or as the filling for a frittata. To make a quesadilla, fill a tortilla with some of the potato mixture and cheese and fold the tortilla in half. Place in a lightly oiled frying pan over medium heat and cook, pressing down on the tortilla with a spatula and turning once, until golden and the cheese is melted.

Preheat the oven to 450°F (230°C). Line a baking sheet with parchment paper.

Put the sweet potatoes in a large bowl. Add the oil, cumin, chili powder, coriander, and salt and toss to coat. Spread in a single layer on the prepared baking sheet. Bake, stirring once about halfway through, until tender and caramelized, 25–30 minutes.

Remove from the oven and stir the chiles into the sweet potatoes on the baking sheet.

To assemble, fill the tortillas with the sweet potato and chile mixture and top with the Monterey jack and a generous drizzle of the crema. Serve right away.

SERVES 4

5 poblano chiles

2 tablespoons canola oil

2 large white onions, halved and cut into ½-inch (12-mm) slices

Kosher salt and freshly ground pepper

2 cloves garlic, minced

1 teaspoon ground cumin

½ teaspoon dried Mexican oregano

8–10 corn or flour tortillas, warmed

Salsa Verde (page 27)

RAJAS POBLANOS TACOS WITH SALSA VERDE

Using tongs or a large fork, hold 1 poblano at a time directly over the flame of a gas burner, or place directly on the grate. Roast, turning as needed, until blistered and charred black on all sides, 10–15 minutes total. (Alternatively, place the poblanos under a preheated broiler, as close as possible to the heating element, and broil to char them on all sides, turning as needed.) Transfer the poblanos to a bowl, cover with plastic wrap or a clean kitchen towel, and set aside to steam until cooled, about 20 minutes. Once cool, peel or rub away the charred skins, then seed the poblanos and cut into strips.

Warm the oil in a large frying pan over high heat. Add the onions, season with salt and pepper, and cook, stirring often, until well browned, 6–8 minutes. Stir in the garlic, cumin, and oregano and sauté just until the garlic is soft, about 2 minutes. Add the poblanos and cook just until the chiles are warmed through, about 2 minutes. Taste and adjust the seasoning.

To assemble, fill the tortillas with the rajas poblanos and serve right away, passing the salsa at the table.

SERVES 4

PEPPERED UP

A classic Mexican taco filling, grilled poblano peppers and onions make for a simple but delicious meal. Poblanos are dark green chiles that are typically roasted, grilled, or stuffed for chiles rellenos. Although a poblano is not a particularly hot chile, you can substitute sweet red and green bell peppers if you want to eliminate the heat altogether.

¼ cup (2 fl oz/60 ml) vegetable oil

1 *each* orange and red bell pepper, seeded and cut into strips

2 small zucchini, quartered lengthwise and cut crosswise into ¼-inch (6-mm) pieces

2 small yellow crookneck squash, quartered lengthwise and cut crosswise into ½-inch (12-mm) pieces

1 tablespoon ground cumin

1 tablespoon chili powder

1 teaspoon kosher salt

10–12 flour or corn tortillas, warmed

1 cup (5 oz/155 g) crumbled queso fresco

Pico de Gallo (page 20)

SUMMER VEGETABLE TACOS WITH QUESO FRESCO

YEAR-ROUND COOKING

⟶ »»»»»»»»

A fast sauté makes this an ideal weeknight dinner. Use this recipe as a guide for other vegetables throughout the year such as sliced mushrooms or chopped kale. Queso fresco means "fresh cheese" and it is a wonderfully salty crumbling cheese for any of your tacos. If you can't find it, feta is an excellent substitution. Complete this summery meal with a Chipotle Caesar Salad (page 121).

Warm the oil in a large frying pan over medium-high heat. Add the bell peppers, zucchini, and squash and stir to coat with the oil. Stir in the cumin, chili powder, and salt and sauté until the vegetables are fork-tender, about 10 minutes.

To assemble, fill the tortillas with the vegetables and top with the queso fresco. Serve right away, passing the pico de gallo at the table.

SERVES 4–6

3 teaspoons olive oil, plus 1 tablespoon

1 small jalapeño chile, thinly sliced

2 cups (12 oz/375 g) cherry tomatoes, halved

2 tablespoons chopped fresh cilantro

Kosher salt and freshly ground pepper

2 large eggs

¼ cup (1½ oz/45 g) all-purpose flour

1 cup (4 oz/125 g) panko bread crumbs

2 firm-but-ripe avocados, pitted, peeled, and each cut into 8 wedges

⅔ cup (5½ oz/170 g) sour cream

2 tablespoons fresh lemon juice

8–10 flour or corn tortillas, warmed

FRIED AVOCADO TACOS WITH TOMATO-JALAPEÑO SALAD

To make the salad, warm 2 teaspoons of the olive oil in a frying pan over medium-high heat. Add the jalapeño and sauté just until soft, about 2 minutes. Transfer to a bowl, add the tomatoes, and drizzle in 1 teaspoon of the olive oil. Add the cilantro, season with salt and pepper, and toss to mix well. Set aside at room temperature until ready to serve.

To fry the avocados, set up an assembly line: In a shallow bowl, beat the eggs. Put the flour in a second shallow bowl next to the eggs and season well with salt and pepper. Put the panko in a third bowl next to the flour. Dip an avocado wedge into the egg, letting the excess drip back into the bowl. Next, dredge the avocado in the seasoned flour, shaking off any excess. Finally, coat the avocado in the panko, making sure to cover on all sides. (Pat the coating gently to help it adhere, if needed.) Transfer to a plate. Repeat to coat the remaining avocado wedges.

Warm the remaining 1 tablespoon olive oil in a nonstick frying pan over medium-high heat. Working in batches as needed to avoid crowding, fry the avocados, carefully turning once, until golden brown on both sides, 3–4 minutes total. Transfer to a plate lined with paper towels to drain.

In a bowl, stir together the sour cream and lemon juice and season with salt. To assemble, fill the tortillas with the avocados, dividing them evenly, and top with a scoop of the tomato salad. Serve right away, passing the lemony sour cream at the table for drizzling.

SERVES 4

FRIED BUT HEALTHY

Panfrying these panko-coated avocado slices makes them seem deliciously indulgent. But you can still feel good about serving them to your family. Loaded in healthy fats and fiber, surrounded by a smattering of fresh vegetables, and served inside a whole grain corn tortilla, these tacos are nutritionally balanced and delicious. Fried avocados are also wonderful tossed in salads or served on top of quesadillas.

1 lb (500 g) Padrón peppers

1 tablespoon olive oil

Juice of ½ lime

Coarse salt

12 corn or flour tortillas, warmed

⅓ lb (155 g) goat cheese, crumbled, at room temperature

¼ cup (⅓ oz/10 g) loosely packed fresh cilantro leaves

Pico de Gallo (page 20)

GRILLED PADRÓN PEPPER & GOAT CHEESE TACOS

FIT FOR DINNER OR A SNACK

Padrón peppers hail from Padrón, Spain. They are small, most often sweet (although every so often you can get a fiery one!), and incredibly juicy and flavorful when grilled and seasoned with salt. If you can't find Padrón peppers, use sweet petite peppers; cut them in half lengthwise after you grill them. Grilled Padrón peppers also make a fantastic appetizer. Serve this dish with a side of grilled chicken or Spicy Pinto Beans (page 103).

Build a hot fire in a charcoal grill or preheat a gas grill to high. Coat the grill grate lightly with cooking spray.

Using kitchen scissors, snip the stem off each pepper. Put the peppers in a large bowl and toss with the olive oil to coat.

Arrange the peppers on the grate directly over the heat and grill, using tongs to turn as needed, until charred on all sides, about 5 minutes total.

Transfer the peppers to the bowl. While they are still hot, drizzle in the lime juice, season generously with salt, and toss to coat thoroughly.

To assemble, fill the tortillas with the peppers and goat cheese, and garnish with big pinches of the cilantro. Serve right away, passing the salsa at the table.

SERVES 6

SIDES & SALADS

2 tablespoons lard or canola oil

½ white onion, finely chopped

2 cloves garlic, minced

1 jalapeño chile, thinly sliced into rings

1 lb (500 g) pinto beans, picked over for stones or grit and rinsed

Kosher salt and freshly ground pepper

1 tablespoon chopped fresh cilantro

SPICY PINTO BEANS

Melt the lard in a large pot with a tight-fitting lid over medium-high heat. Add the onion and sauté until soft and golden brown, 6–8 minutes. Add the garlic and jalapeño and sauté just until soft, about 1 minute. Add the beans and enough cold water to cover by 2 inches (5 cm).

Bring the water to a boil, then reduce the heat to low, cover, and simmer until the beans are tender, about 2½ hours. Check the pot once in a while to make sure that the beans are still covered with water, adding a little more if needed.

Uncover the pot and season the beans with salt and pepper. (You may be surprised by how much salt you need to add to get the flavors to pop.) Cook, uncovered, for about 20 minutes to allow the sauce to thicken and the seasonings to blend. Transfer to a bowl, add the cilantro, and serve right away.

SERVES 6–8

DINNER OR A SIDE

While these beans are delicious inside tacos, they are also flavorful enough to serve on their own. For a simple supper, serve these savory beans on a bed of Arroz Blanco (page 117) and top with crumbled queso fresco and cubes of creamy, ripe avocado.

2 tablespoons lard, bacon drippings, or canola oil

½ white onion, finely chopped

3 cloves garlic, minced

1 teaspoon ground cumin

Kosher salt and freshly ground pepper

2 cans (15 oz/470 g each) black beans, rinsed and drained

¾ cup (6 fl oz/180 ml) low-sodium chicken or vegetable broth

OAXACAN BLACK BEANS

PANTRY STAPLE

——→→→→→→→→→→

Canned beans are an easy fix for a last-minute dinner, so keep them on hand in your pantry. Since they aren't seasoned, cooking them with onion, garlic, and broth will add terrific flavor. For a pretty presentation, top black beans with a dollop of sour cream and lemon zest. Serve these alongside Tequila-Lime Chicken Tacos with Radish-Avocado Salad (page 56).

Melt the lard in a heavy-bottomed saucepan over medium-high heat. Add the onion and sauté until translucent, about 5 minutes. Stir in the garlic and cumin, season with salt and pepper, and sauté just until the garlic is soft, about 1 minute.

Add the beans and stir to coat with the fat and seasonings. Add the broth, stir once or twice, and bring to a boil. Reduce the heat to low and simmer until the beans thicken, about 20 minutes. Taste and adjust the seasoning. Let beans rest for 10 minutes then serve right away.

SERVES 4–6

1 lb (500 g) pinto beans, picked over
for stones or grit and rinsed

2 tablespoons lard or canola oil

1 white onion, finely chopped

4 cloves garlic, minced

Kosher salt and freshly ground pepper

REFRIED BEANS

Put the beans in a large pot with a tight-fitting lid over medium-high heat and add cold water to cover by 2 inches (5 cm). Bring to a boil, then reduce the heat to low, cover, and simmer until the beans are tender, about 2½ hours. Check the pot once in a while to make sure that the beans are still covered with water, adding a little more if needed. Strain the beans, reserving the cooking liquid.

Melt the lard in a large frying pan over medium-high heat. Add the onion and sauté until golden brown, 8–10 minutes. Add the garlic and cook just until soft, about 1 minute. Add about ¼ cup (2 oz/60 g) of the beans and, using a potato masher, smash them into a coarse purée. Continue to add beans a generous ¼ cup at a time, mashing as you go.

When all of the beans have been added, pour in ¾ cup (6 fl oz/180 ml) of the bean-cooking liquid and stir to mix well. Stir in a little more of the liquid to achieve the consistency you like, if needed. Season with salt and pepper and serve right away.

SERVES 6–8

AUTHENTIC BEANS

Here's the recipe for the real deal! Of course, if you are short on time, the canned version is also delicious. The beans in this recipe will thicken as they cool, so keep your cooking liquid on hand until you are ready to serve. You can add more liquid as needed to achieve the perfect texture.

4 ears of corn

2 tablespoons unsalted butter, melted

CORN ON THE COB THREE WAYS

THE ULTIMATE SIDE

>>>>>>>>>>

When corn is in season, there is no better side dish. Here are three ways to dress up your ears, and each of them would shine at a backyard barbecue. You can either boil or grill the corn in this recipe. The only trick is that you should season the corn while it is still hot so that the ingredients adhere to the corn, giving you maximum flavor.

FOR GRILLED CORN Build a medium-hot fire in a charcoal grill or preheat a gas grill to medium-high. Keeping the stalk intact, remove all but a few of the outer husks from the corn cobs. Arrange the corn on the grate directly over the heat and grill, using tongs to rotate every couple of minutes, until blackened in spots all over, about 8 minutes. Transfer the corn to a platter and let cool briefly, then remove the remaining husks and silks from each ear (alternatively, pull back the remaining husks and use a husk to tie in place). Season the corn as desired (see below).

FOR BOILED CORN Bring a large pot of lightly salted water to a boil. Remove the husks and silks from the corn and carefully drop into the boiling water. Cook until fork-tender, about 8 minutes. Using tongs, transfer to a colander and let drain, then transfer to a platter and let sit for about 10 seconds to allow any water clinging to the ears to evaporate. Season the corn as desired (see below).

Once you have grilled or boiled the corn, immediately brush the corn with the melted butter and sprinkle with one of the toppings below, as you like. Serve right away.

SPICY In a small bowl, stir together 2 teaspoons chili powder; 1 teaspoon ground cumin; ½ teaspoon kosher salt; and ¼ teaspoon cayenne pepper.

PARMESAN & LIME In a small bowl, stir together 5 tablespoons (1¼ oz/40 g) finely grated Parmesan cheese; zest of 2 limes; and ½ teaspoon kosher salt.

COTIJA & CILANTRO In a small bowl, stir together 1 cup (5 oz/155 g) finely crumbled cotija cheese; ½ cup (¾ oz/20 g) loosely packed fresh cilantro leaves, finely chopped; and ¼ teaspoon kosher salt.

SERVES 4

1 poblano chile

1 clove garlic

1 teaspoon Dijon mustard

⅓ cup (3 fl oz/80 ml) fresh orange juice (from 1 or 2 oranges)

1 tablespoon red wine vinegar

½ teaspoon kosher salt

⅛ teaspoon freshly ground pepper

3 teaspoons extra-virgin olive oil

6 cups (6 oz/185 g) loosely packed arugula leaves

2 oranges, peel and pith removed, cut into half-moon shapes

¼ small jicama, peeled and cut into matchsticks (about ½ cup/2 oz/60 g)

2 tablespoons roasted and salted pumpkin seeds

ARUGULA SALAD WITH JICAMA, ORANGES & PUMPKIN SEEDS

To make the dressing, using tongs or a large fork, hold the chile directly over the flame of a gas burner, or place directly on the grate. Roast, turning as needed, until blistered and charred black on all sides, 10–15 minutes total. (Alternatively, place the chile under a preheated broiler, as close as possible to the heating element, and broil to char on all sides, turning as needed.) Transfer the chile to a bowl, cover with plastic wrap or a clean kitchen towel, and set aside to steam until cooled, about 20 minutes. Once cool, peel or rub away the charred skin, then seed the chile and chop.

Combine the chile, garlic, mustard, orange juice, vinegar, salt, and pepper in a food processor or blender. Process to a smooth purée. With the machine running, drizzle in the olive oil in a slow, steady stream and process until well blended.

In a large bowl, toss the arugula with the dressing to taste. Add the oranges, jicama, and pumpkin seeds and toss to combine. Taste and adjust the seasoning. Serve right away.

SERVES 4

FRESH & EASY

Refreshing and sweet, this fully loaded salad comes together in minutes. To save even more time, the dressing can be made ahead of time and stored in the refrigerator for 1 week. The dressing is delicious on other combinations of salads, or drizzled atop Arroz Blanco (page 117). Serve this salad alongside Grilled Red Snapper Tacos with Mexican Chimichurri (page 76) for a stand-out meal.

1/3 cup (3 fl oz/80 ml) fresh lime juice (from about 3 limes)

1 teaspoon honey

1 teaspoon ground cumin

1/2 teaspoon kosher salt

Pinch of cayenne pepper

2 tablespoons extra-virgin olive oil

1 large head butter lettuce, torn into bite-sized pieces (about 6 cups/6 oz/185 g)

1/4 papaya, peeled, seeded, and cut into small cubes

1 ripe avocado, pitted, peeled, and sliced

1/4 red onion, thinly sliced

BUTTER LETTUCE, PAPAYA & AVOCADO SALAD

MAKE IT A MEAL

→→→→→→→→

A refreshing salad is always a good choice to accompany a spicy taco dinner and this one hits all the high points. For a salad hearty enough to call dinner, top this one with the filling from the skirt steak tacos (page 38) or the ancho chili chicken tacos (page 54). Or, serve this salad with a Monterey jack cheese quesadilla.

To make the vinaigrette, in a small bowl, whisk together the lime juice, honey, cumin, salt, and cayenne. Slowly drizzle in the olive oil, whisking until well blended. Taste and adjust the seasoning.

In a large bowl, toss the lettuce with the vinaigrette to taste. Transfer to a serving platter or large, shallow serving bowl. Garnish with the papaya, avocado, and onion. Serve right away.

SERVES 4

1 or 2 chipotle chiles in adobo sauce, minced

3 tablespoons pure maple syrup

1 tablespoon canola oil

½ teaspoon kosher salt

1 lb (500 g) sweet potatoes, peeled and cut into ¼-inch (6-mm) dice

CHIPOTLE & MAPLE-ROASTED SWEET POTATOES

Preheat the oven to 450°F (230°C). Coat a baking sheet lightly with cooking spray.

Put the chipotle chile or chiles (depending on how spicy you'd like your potatoes) in a large bowl. Add the maple syrup, oil, and salt and whisk to mix well. Add the sweet potatoes and toss to coat.

Spread the sweet potatoes in a single layer on the prepared baking sheet. Bake, stirring once, until tender and caramelized, 25–30 minutes. Serve right away.

SERVES 4

VERSATILE SIDE

A tasty combination of spicy and sweet, this vegetable side dish is delicious alongside tacos. The roasted sweet potatoes also make a good filling; roll them up in warm tortillas and top with a dollop of sour cream. Since the recipe calls for just a small amount of the chipotle chiles, store the rest in a small airtight container in the freezer for up to 1 month.

1½ tablespoons unsalted butter, at room temperature

Zest of 1 lemon and 1 tablespoon fresh lemon juice

Kosher salt and freshly ground pepper

1 lb (500 g) asparagus, tough woody ends snapped or cut off

STEAMED ASPARAGUS WITH LEMON BUTTER

STEAMED OR GRILLED

>>>>>>>>>>

Simple and fast, this dish will pair with all kinds of weeknight dinners in addition to tacos. If you are grilling tacos, add the asparagus to the grill then toss with the lemon butter. Try the lemon butter on different vegetables throughout the year including broccoli, roasted mushrooms, and bok choy.

In a large bowl, stir together the butter and lemon zest and juice. Season with salt and pepper. Set aside.

Pour water into a large, wide pot with a tight-fitting lid to a depth of 1 inch (2.5 cm). Salt the water generously and fit a steamer basket in the bottom of the pot. Bring to a boil over high heat. When the water is boiling, add the asparagus to the steamer, reduce the heat to medium, and cover the pot. Steam the asparagus until just fork-tender, about 5 minutes.

Using tongs, transfer the hot asparagus to the bowl with the lemon butter toss to coat with the butter. Transfer to a serving platter and serve right away.

SERVES 4

WHAT YOU NEED

2½ cups (20 fl oz/625 ml) low-sodium chicken or vegetable broth

2 tablespoons olive oil

½ white onion, finely chopped

2 cloves garlic, minced

1 teaspoon ground cumin

Kosher salt and freshly ground pepper

1 cup (7 oz/220 g) white rice

2 tablespoons finely chopped fresh cilantro

ARROZ BLANCO

Warm the broth in a small saucepan over medium heat.

Meanwhile, warm the oil in a heavy-bottomed saucepan with a tight-fitting lid over medium-high heat. Add the onion and sauté until translucent, about 5 minutes. Stir in the garlic and cumin, season with salt and pepper, and sauté just until the garlic is soft, about 1 minute.

Add the rice to the pan with the onion and garlic and stir to coat with the oil and seasonings. Add the warmed broth and bring to a boil. Cover, reduce the heat to low, and simmer until the liquid is absorbed, about 20 minutes.

Remove from the heat and stir in the cilantro. Taste and adjust the seasoning. Serve right away.

SERVES 4

CUMIN-SCENTED RICE

When rice cooks in broth it takes on a sophisticated flavor, making it a highlight on the table, rather than a filler. This dish gets an extra boost from onion, garlic, and cumin. The trick to getting light and fluffy rice is to make sure your pot has a tight-fitting lid and resist the urge to peek at the rice as it cooks.

1 small seedless watermelon, 4–5 lb (2–2.5 kg)

Zest and juice of 1 lime

⅓ lb (155 g) feta cheese, crumbled

6 fresh mint leaves, julienned

WATERMELON & FETA SALAD WITH MINT & LIME

COOLING TREAT

→→→→→→→→→

An enticing combination of sweet, salty, and sour flavors comes together in this fruit-forward salad. It's especially delicious with spicy tacos, so try it with Chipotle Turkey Tacos with Refried Beans (page 58) or Chorizo, Potato & Spinach Tacos (page 47). Don't chop the mint until you are ready to serve as it will turn brown around the edges.

Cut both ends off the watermelon and stand up on one end. Using a chef's knife and following the contour of the fruit, cut away the rind, including all of the white flesh, until you are left with only the melon. Turn the watermelon on its side and cut into 1-inch (2.5-cm) slices, then lay the slices flat and cut into ½-inch (12-mm) cubes.

Transfer the watermelon to a serving platter. Sprinkle the lime zest and juice all over the watermelon. Toss gently with your hands to mix.

Garnish with the feta and mint and serve right away.

SERVES 6–8

¼ cup (2 fl oz/60 ml) fresh lemon juice

¼ cup (1 oz/30 g) freshly grated Parmesan cheese, plus more for garnish

1 small chipotle chile in adobo sauce, minced

1 clove garlic, minced

½ cup (4 fl oz/125 ml) extra-virgin olive oil, plus 1 tablespoon

Kosher salt and freshly ground pepper

1 tablespoon unsalted butter

3 slices peasant or other crusty, rustic bread, cut into ½-inch (12-mm) cubes (about 1½ cups/3 oz/90 g)

1 large head romaine lettuce, cut into bite-sized pieces (about 6 cups/6 oz/185 g)

CHIPOTLE CAESAR SALAD

To make the dressing, in a small bowl, whisk together the lemon juice, Parmesan, chipotle chile, and garlic. Slowly drizzle in the ½ cup olive oil, whisking until well blended. Season with salt and pepper. Set aside.

Melt the butter with the 1 tablespoon olive oil in a large frying pan over medium-high heat. Add the bread cubes and toss to coat with the butter and oil. Season well with salt and pepper and cook, stirring occasionally, until toasted all over, about 6 minutes.

To assemble, in a large salad bowl, toss the lettuce with the dressing to taste. Garnish with the croutons and Parmesan. Serve right away.

SERVES 4

A NEW CLASSIC

This spicy riff on the original is a fun addition to a Mexican themed dinner. You can control the amount of heat you want by adding more or less of the chipotle chile. The dressing can be made a few days ahead but the croutons are best hot out of the frying pan. To turn this salad into a full meal, top it with blackened salmon (page 71), tequila-lime chicken (page 56), or chili-rubbed shrimp (page 67).

MENUS

From busy weeknights with kids to entertaining guests on a Saturday, planning a delicious, balanced dinner is a cinch with these menus as your guide. For tips on planning a dinner timeline, see page 12.

MEATLESS MONDAY

Fast and nutritious, this light meal is loaded with flavor.

BEANS & GREENS TACO (page 85)
GRILLED PADRÓN PEPPER & GOAT CHEESE TACOS (page 98)
ARROZ BLANCO (page 117)
FOR THE ADULTS Cold beer
FOR THE KIDS Sparkling water with lemon and lime

MEXICAN FIESTA

These tasty, colorful dishes are terrific for entertaining.

CHICKEN TACO NACHOS (page 62)
BUTTER LETTUCE, PAPAYA & AVOCADO SALAD (page 112)
**WATERMELON & FETA SALAD WITH
  MINT & LIME** (page 118)
FOR THE ADULTS Margaritas
FOR THE KIDS Strawberry or watermelon aguas frescas

DINNER FOR TWO

Pair these elegant dishes with a cool bottle of wine for a memorable meal.

**PAN-SEARED SCALLOPS WITH
  MEYER LEMON–CILANTRO AIOLI** (page 72)
**ARUGULA SALAD WITH JICAMA, ORANGES
  & PUMPKIN SEEDS** (page 109)
FOR THE ADULTS Chilled rosé

HEARTY & HEALTHY

These fueling tacos provide lots of vegetables and nutrients.

**ROASTED BUTTERNUT SQUASH, SPINACH
  & BLACK BEAN TACOS** (page 86)
**FRIED AVOCADO TACOS WITH
  TOMATO–JALAPEÑO SALAD** (page 97)
FOR THE KIDS & ADULTS Sparkling water with lemon and lime

GRILL NIGHT

Fire up the grill! Tonight the whole meal gets charred and smoky for a crowd-pleasing dinner.

**GRILLED RED SNAPPER TACOS WITH
  MEXICAN CHIMICHURRI** (page 76)
GRILLED CORN & ZUCCHINI TACOS (page 89)
CORN ON THE COB THREE WAYS (page 106)
FOR THE ADULTS Cold beer
FOR THE KIDS Sparkling lemonade

BREAKFAST FOR DINNER

What could be more fun than breakfast for dinner? Try a make-your-own breakfast taco bar.

BREAKFAST SOFT TACOS (page 43)
CHIPOTLE & MAPLE-ROASTED SWEET POTATOES (page 115)
FOR THE ADULTS Mimosas
FOR THE KIDS Freshly squeezed orange juice

INDEX

weldonowen

415 Jackson Street, Suite 200, San Francisco, CA 94111
www.weldonowen.com

TACO NIGHT
Conceived and produced by Weldon Owen, Inc.
In collaboration with Williams-Sonoma, Inc.
3250 Van Ness Avenue, San Francisco, CA 94109

A WELDON OWEN PRODUCTION

Printed and bound in China by 1010 Printing, Ltd.

First printed in 2014
10 9 8 7 6 5 4 3 2 1

Library of Congress Control Number: 2014943773

ISBN 13: 978-1-61628-733-7
ISBN 10: 1-61628-733-0

Weldon Owen is a division of
BONNIER

WELDON OWEN, INC
CEO and President Terry Newell
VP, Sales and Marketing Amy Kaneko
VP, Publisher Roger Shaw
Finance Director Philip Paulick

Associate Publisher Amy Marr
Assistant Editor Emma Rudolph

Creative Director Kelly Booth
Senior Production Designer Rachel Lopez Metzger

Production Director Chris Hemesath
Associate Production Director Michelle Duggan

Photographer Erin Kunkel
Food Stylist Erin Quon
Prop Stylist Leigh Noe

ACKNOWLEDGEMENTS
Weldon Owen wishes to thank the following people for
their generous support in producing this book:
Kris Balloun, David Bornfriend, Marisa Kwek, Kim Laidlaw, Ashley Lima
Chuck Luter, Lori Nunokawa, Elizabeth Parson, and Sharon Silva